INSPIRING OTHERS

TO

WIN

Edited by

Robert B. Sommer

Griffin Publishing Group
Glendale, California

Editorial Statement

In the interest of brevity and unencumbered prose, the editor has chosen to use the standard English form of address. This usage is not meant to suggest that the content of this book, both in its references and to whom it is addressed, is intended as restrictive or exclusive regarding any individual or group of individuals, whether by gender, race, age, or any other means that might be considered discriminatory.

Publisher: Robert Howland
Director of Operations: Robin Howland
Managing Editor: Marjorie L. Marks
Book Design: Mark M. Dodge
Cover Design: Big Fish

10 9 8 7 6 5 4 3 2 1

ISBN 1-882180-94-1

For more information about the authors in this publication, please contact Best of the Masters. Additional Olympic-related materials are available from Griffin Publishing Group.

Griffin Publishing Group
544 West Colorado Street
Glendale, CA 91204
Phone: (818) 244-1470
Fax: (818) 244-7408

Best of the Masters
6361 Yarrow Ave., Suite C
Carlsbad, CA 92009
Phone: (800) 356-3338

Manufactured in the United States of America

FOREWORD

For as long as I can remember I have been dedicated to personal and physical development. Precisely what portion of my motivation existed at the time of my birth and what portion was added along the way remains a mystery to me. This much, however, is clear; natural drive increases relative to one's exposure to inspiration. That may sound simple, but inspiration doesn't just happen the way rain falls upon the sidewalk. In order to absorb inspiration, one must truly be open to it. Perhaps a better analogy is the way in which flowers and plants turn themselves toward a source of light, stretching themselves in order to soak up more natural material that, in turn, increases their ability to grow.

In retrospect, I can see that that was my own method for enhancing my motivation to become a better wrestler. At the age of ten I decided I wanted to win an Olympic Gold Medal. Along the way, I collected and stored inspiration from as many speakers, books and coaches as I could. Dedication to the sport of wrestling culminated in my winning the Olympic Gold Medal in freestyle wrestling at the 1960 Olympic Games in Rome.

Since all journeys lead to other journeys, my quest for personal growth did not end there, nor did my search for inspiration. Upon my return from Rome, I was asked to speak before numerous audiences about my Olympic experience. As I did so, I discovered a new challenge to grapple with. Following one of my appearances, I confided in a friend that I wasn't satisfied with my speaking ability. My friend suggested that I join Toastmasters.*

Again my drive was ignited, this time toward a whole world of personal growth and learning. Along this road, I encountered a wealth of inspiration in the form of my supportive fellow Toastmasters.

I feel fortunate to have followed this path because, by transferring my determination to succeed to the public speaking and leadership opportunities that Toastmasters provides, I continually find myself prepared to take on ever-increasing challenges. Moreover, Toastmasters allows me to continually discover new sources of inspiration from the words and accomplishments of a broad range of people. To me, that is the beauty of inspiration—it is wholly transferable to anyone, in any arena or endeavor. In turn, I have learned how to participate more fully in this exchange by working to inspire others. Perhaps that has been my greatest challenge yet. Certainly it has been the most rewarding. Readers, too, will find themselves rewarded. To absorb true inspiration, and to learn how to give it, they need only open themselves to the illuminations that glow from the pages of *Inspiring Others to Win!*

—Terrence J. McCann
Olympic Gold Medalist and
Executive Director, Toastmasters International

*Toastmasters International offers a safe, inexpensive and proven way to practice your newly developed speaking skills in a supportive environment. Most cities in the United States have several Toastmasters clubs that meet at various times and locations throughout each week. If you are interested in forming or joining a Toastmasters club in your community or your company, call 714-858-8255. For a listing of local clubs, call 800-9WE SPEAK or write Toastmasters International, P.O. Box 9052, Mission Viejo, CA 92690. You can also visit our Web page at www.toastmasters.org.

CONTENTS

INTRODUCTION

Robert B. Sommer
800-356-3338
760-929-1019
somrob@aol.com

Rob Sommer has been working with professional speakers, trainers and consultants since 1983. His background in advertising, marketing and video production has been invaluable in the production of audio and video products as well as in the publication of books and newsletters.

The American Spirit has always glowed upon hearing the word "win." It speaks of freedom, dedication and personal initiative. Our society reveres those who have overcome their challenges and made their dreams a reality. This is a book about inspiring people to do just that: to dream, to persist, to win.

This remarkable collection of authors includes athletes, business leaders, media personalities, educators and high achievers of many types. What they have in common is their continuing commitment to pass along to others what they have successfully applied in their own lives. All of these professional speakers are people whose careers are now focused on *inspiring others to win.*

In these pages they will show you how to use the techniques that work so well for them. You'll discover the master strategies for leading and motivating people to be all that they can be. Through their messages you will gain new wings to lift others to the heights of their own potential.

I commend you on what you are about to learn.

—Robert B. Sommer
President, Best of the Masters

DAILY OPPORTUNITIES TO INSPIRE

Jim Cathcart,
CSP, CPAE
800-222-4883
619-456-3813
Jim@Cathcart.com
www.cathcart.com

The author is celebrating twenty-one years of helping people grow their businesses and expand their lives through his speeches, seminars, books, tapes and consulting services. Jim Cathcart is the author of *Relationship Selling and the Acorn Principle*. He served as the 1988-89 President of the National Speakers Association. Cathcart's new book, *The Acorn Principle, Nurture Your Nature* (St. Martin's Press, Sept. 1998), is a guide to conducting a complete "life checkup" and learning how to nurture the strengths and possibilities within yourself.

It is one of the great compensations of life that no man can sincerely endeavor to help another without, in turn, helping himself.

—Ralph Waldo Emerson

Ron was dining alone when the older couple was seated at a table nearby. As he finished his meal he noticed that these people were truly enjoying each other's company. They told each other stories, laughed, flirted. It was fun to watch. Though clearly in their eighties they seemed to give each other youth.

On his way out Ron said to them, "Excuse me. I don't wish to intrude but I'd like to offer an observation. I've been noticing you both from across the room. And I must say that you are either very young lovers, very dear friends or you just have a truly special relationship."

Upon hearing this, the couple became wonderfully radiant. Smiles erupted on their faces as they shared a joyful glance. "What a delightful thing to say!" they told him. "Please join us."

The offer was sincere but Ron politely declined and bid them goodbye. Both Ron and the couple were smiling warmly as he exited the restaurant.

When Ron told me this story he said, "Jim, the beauty of this experience was my own surprise at how wonderful it made *me* feel! I never expected that."

Studies repeatedly have proven that people who give of themselves for others live longer, stay healthier and do their work more effectively than those who don't reach out to help. Our culture is experiencing an all-time high in charitable giving and volunteer service. People are discovering the joy of helping. One of the wonderful side benefits of helping is that it is contagious.

Ask any successful person "Who has helped or inspired you along the way?" You'll see them smile as they recall those who influenced them. Some stories are of direct relationships with friends, parents or coaches. Others are stories of how the words, deeds or examples set by others have in turn inspired them to win. Their influence conveyed the message, "You can do it!"

Now answer the question for yourself: "Who has helped or inspired you?"

In 1972 I worked as a government clerk, an assistant loan specialist at the Little Rock, Arkansas Housing Authority. My pay was $525 a month and my job required very few hours of effort each day. I was frustrated in my desire to succeed. As a new father, 26, with no college degree or business "connections" my options seemed very limited.

Then one day I heard a radio program called "Our Changing World." Its narrator was Earl Nightingale, a man known worldwide as "the Dean of personal motivation."

In his broadcast that day Nightingale said, "If you will spend one hour (extra) each day in study in your field...you'll be a national expert in five years or less." "Five years or less?", I thought, "Heck, I'm a government clerk. I've got eight free hours a day. I could do this by Thursday!"

His message inspired me. Suddenly I could see a path for becoming more significant and more successful. But I had one remaining problem: I didn't want to be an urban renewal expert at the Housing Authority.

As I thought of Earl Nightingale's words in the ensuing weeks, however, I realized that what I really wanted to do was what *he* was doing. I wanted to help people grow.

So I began to study books, tapes, seminars, other people, anything from which I could learn. It took me a full five years of hard, dedicated learning but, sure enough, I ultimately became a speaker, trainer and author who was helping people to grow.

Earl Nightingale and I met in person only once, at a motivational rally in 1977. We spoke on the phone on three other occasions. He never got to know me as a person, yet both his works and his personal example had inspired me to win.

ᵹᴑ

Bill Wesso was a braggart. He boasted about how smart he was, about his physical skills, even about the car he drove. Yet despite his annoying behavior, Bill Wesso also inspired me to win. The year was 1964. I was in high school. I encountered Bill every day, in class, in the gymnasium, after school, everywhere. One day his bragging just became too much for me. I decided to call his hand. So I challenged him and his "fast car" to a drag race. Not just any drag race, a very unique one.

Bill drove a Mercury Park Lane Marauder. It was a huge car with a huge engine. He claimed it was faster than anyone's. So I called his bluff. I said, "Wesso, not only is my car faster than yours. I am faster than your car. I challenge you and your car to a drag race...but the catch is, I will be racing you on foot!

He laughed an embarrassing laugh and then accepted my challenge right there in front of all our classmates. The entire school buzzed about the event. On the appointed day scores of us met at the local drag strip and awaited the contest.

We had agreed to race a total of sixteen car lengths, the exact length of a bridge at the start of the track. I lined up on the left and Bill's car was on the right. When the flagman dropped his flag, Bill floored his accelerator and I started sprinting with all I had. His engine roared, his tires squealed and I was puffing and running as fast as I could. The pounding of my feet on the pavement matched the pounding of my heart. I felt the end of the race was near but all I could see was a cloud of dust and exhaust fumes from Bill's car. With my last bit of breath I pushed myself across the finish line, a nose ahead of the car. The crowd was cheering for me.

This contest was, of course, ridiculous. It didn't matter to anyone but those of us involved. But despite our silliness, Bill Wesso had inspired me to compete and win. He did so in a very negative way and my response was a juvenile one.

Yet, *it is worthwhile to acknowledge how much influence we have on each other's lives.* We never know what effect our behaviors will have on others. But we do know that our behavior counts—both positively and negatively.

My eloquent friend Naomi Rhode, who, like me, is a past president of the National Speakers Association, says in an intentional double-negative statement, "You can't *not* lead by example." In other words, succeed or fail, try or neglect, care or don't...you are always influencing others via your example.

We say to children, "Do as I say, not as I do." Then they do as we do instead of as we say. They follow our examples more often than our words.

There are many ways to inspire others through our actions. We can...

- Do as we wish others would do.
- Show them simple steps to follow in order to win.
- Believe in them more than they believe in themselves.

- Describe the future possibilities in vivid stories.
- Pose provocative questions like, "What could happen if you merely did this?"
- Challenge them to stretch their thinking and reach for bigger possibilities.
- Point out strengths they don't know they have.
- Coach and counsel them as they grow.
- Introduce them to great ideas, books, teachers and sources of information.
- Be their friend even when they are not noticeably succeeding.
- Refuse to tolerate laziness, negligence, or low standards of behavior in them or us.
- Appeal to their desire to be a better person.
- Remind them that pain, fear and disappointment are simply momentary steps on the road to success.
- Nudge them and remind them of the good things they could do or achieve.
- Show them how their behavior has value to others, that they matter in the world.
- Point out better ways for them to apply their talents and be of greater service to others.

There are many ways to inspire others and all of them have their time and place. The beauty of this is that as we do these things for others, we inspire ourselves as well.

There are eight elements necessary for a person to be truly empowered to win. I call these the "Eight T's".

Target—Know where you want to go and why. There must be a clear goal, dream or outcome that directs one's energies toward improvement. Until there is a clear target, our energies are dissipated and weakened through lack of focus.

Tools—Get the tools necessary to do the job well. Without the right tools, even the best artist, technician or performer would be less than they could be. Imagine attempting to build a business without a telephone or computer. With the best tools, they can be more than anyone imagined. Think of what the Internet has done for researchers.

Training—Learn how to put the tools to their highest and best use. Teach them how to think about their task and how to master their craft. Talent without training will not produce skill.

Time—Take enough time to do it right. Sometimes training takes a while to sink in. Let them grow into the mastery they need. Provide the opportunity to test and develop new abilities while keeping risk to a minimum.

Truth—Show them the ways in which they and their performance fit into the overall scheme. Those who only know "how" will almost always work for those who also know "why." The more you know the higher you can go.

Trust—Give them room to grow. Trust them enough to allow them to exert initiative but not so much that you create great risk. Nothing advances until somebody does more than they have done before. And nobody does more than they have done before until someone else trusts them enough to give them the room to experiment and grow.

Tracking—Winners always know the score. Create a situation where they know at all times whether they are on track or not. Let them keep their own scorecard too. As professional speaker and author Dr. Ken Blanchard says, "Feedback is the breakfast of champions."

Touch—Celebrate their victories, help them learn from their failures and inspire them to grow. Everything worthwhile is done within the context of a relationship. Without the "human touch," which includes support, encouragement and caring feedback, there is no will to persist.

With this checklist you can easily determine which elements are needed to complete the mix. A person who has all eight "T's" truly is in a position to be self-directed.

Think of someone you would like to inspire. What do you want to inspire them to do, specifically? Now look at the list of Eight T's and determine which elements are missing. With this exercise your next steps should become obvious. Work to provide all eight elements and inspiration will come.

Years ago my son, Jim, Jr., asked me to teach him to play the guitar. This was before I understood the Eight T's. My response was predictable, at least for a typical motivational speaker. I created an elaborate three-year plan. I gave him my spare guitar, a book of chords, outlined a series of daily exercises, and booked him for several sessions with a local guitar instructor. It was as if he had requested a drink of water and I replied with a blast from a fire hose! He promptly lost interest in playing the guitar.

Years later when he was off at college, a friend asked if he was interested in learning guitar. After making sure that I was nowhere around, Jim, Jr. responded, "Sure!" His friend then asked, "What's your favorite song?" Then he taught Jim how to play that song. With this clear reason to learn how to play, Jim practiced consistently until he had mastered the song. Then he learned another, and another. He ultimately went to a guitar instructor on his own and has spent hundreds of hours in disciplined study of music.

Today, many years later, my son is an accomplished guitarist and songwriter. He can even sit in front of the radio and accurately play along with the recordings. And to cap it off, when he comes home for holiday visits, he teaches me guitar techniques! The student has become the master.

My primitive attempt to teach him guitar might have worked for some but certainly not for him, even though he had requested the instruction. His friend's more enlightened approach to teaching used the Eight T's more effectively. He clarified the *Target*, learning a favorite song. He loaned Jim the *Tools*, a guitar on which to practice and a book of chords, and musical instruction. He supervised and coached the practice, the *Training*. He allowed plenty of *Time* for the learning to take place.

There was an atmosphere of *Truth* conducive to learning. There was no father to impress or grades to be earned. The *Tracking* was automatic. Jim, Jr. knew when he did not achieve the desired result by listening to his own playing and watching the reactions of his instructor. He *Trusted* Jim to make his own decisions since the risk was virtually nonexistent if he made a mistake. Finally, his friend provided the human *Touch*. He applauded the successes and corrected the failures. Then as Jim Jr. progressed, even others gave him feedback (more *Tracking*) and support.

Think of a skill that you have developed. Aren't there many parallels between the foregoing example and your own learning experience? The principles that helped you grow and that allowed me to advance in my chosen field are the same principles that apply to sports, competition, education and art. *Techniques may vary from one situation to the next, but principles never change. Learn the principles and you can devise your own techniques.*

You and I are daily provided with opportunities to help others grow. We see the potential of others more clearly than they do. We sense opportunities that escape their notice. With the simple principles in this chapter, you can make a major impact on the advancement of others. You can inspire them to win—and in so doing, no doubt, you will also inspire yourself.

℘

2

ONE PERSON CAN MAKE A DIFFERENCE:

INSPIRING BY COACHING

Niki & Dennis McCuistion, CSPs
800-543-0310
972-255-2599
mccuisti@ix.netcom.com
www.mccuistiontv.com

A team committed to making a difference through education and "helping companies and individuals develop and implement strategies for change."

The McCuistion firm is celebrating its twenty-first year in business.

Dennis, a bank CEO, at age 29 specializes in strategy, change management, economic and financial issues. His speaking blends humor with serious content and how-to's. Dennis is host of the McCuistion TV program, now in its eighth year on PBS and on cable stations throughout the country.

Niki produces the award-winning McCuistion program, voted by the Dallas Observer, "1997's Most Informative Local Public Issues Broadcast." Her speaking programs are researched and tailored to meet her client's strategic needs in leadership, customer service and sales and executive coaching.

The letter was unexpected. I held it in my hand, weighing it, looking at the return address, the handwriting. Then I turned it over and laid it down. Finally, curiosity got the best of me.

"I wanted to share something with you," it read. "The other day I went to write in my journal, the one you gave me, and decided to read some of what I had written. It's filled with my goals, as well as many of the things you and I had talked about. I wish you could truly know how much those ideas meant to me."

"I just wanted you to know that I will always look at you as someone to look up to. I'd like to keep in touch but feel kind of bad after all that's happened. You and Dennis have both contributed to helping me grow in lots of ways."

"You'll be proud to know we're out of debt, have saved money and are building a house. It's our first, and as you might guess, we're excited. We'd like to have you over for dinner as two of our first guests."

"We're doing well, working hard, going to church and dreaming about a business of our own to help other families in trouble. The kids are doing great at school, you'd be so proud. My daughter's teacher complimented me the other day on how well the kids are doing. Thank you so very much, for all you've done. You and Dennis taught me so much..." The letter went on for several pages.

When Niki finished reading and was able to put the letter down, the room was dark. She had been lost in thought without realizing that time had flown by. The letter had prompted memories, some painful, some bittersweet. Its sender had been a trusted employee for several years but we finally had parted ways.

Barbara (not her real name) had been a good worker when she wanted to be, but her personal life had been a shambles. She was on the verge of separating, she and her husband were dangerously in debt and they had been going to counseling with no success. She had alienated her co-workers, her own work was suffering, and it was rough going for everyone concerned.

We had worked with her for months, coaching and sometimes counseling. To accommodate her we'd gone on flex time and even that had been taken advantage of. We'd finally had to throw in the towel.

Had Barbara truly changed? She sounded transformed. Had we been instrumental in this change through our coaching and mentoring? Barbara seemed to think so. We'd mentored and coached others before, yet the results Barbara had outlined were impressive.

Our curiosity was aroused. Was the outcome achieved as a result of the coaching and mentoring one of us (more than the other), had been responsible for or was the coaching process successful only to the extent that the student or the mentee was ready to accept the message? Yes to both.

That question a year or so ago, and the letter that prompted it led to extensive study, with one of us enrolled in a masters program, with the intent to revise most of her work and redirect it toward coaching and leadership. It has also led to a new focus in our consulting work with very successful results. Our PBS television program, "McCuistion: Talking About Things That Matter With People Who Care," has featured programs on coaching and peak performance, all because of one person, one letter later!

An accident, an isolated incident? We don't think so. We just don't always hear back from the people we coach and mentor. Good coaching and mentoring, *consistently* done, can produce tremendous results for an individual and his or her performance and outlook. It can successfully turn around a life and the lives of others whom it touches.

That evening as we talked about the letter, Barbara's new life, and our hand at helping it along, we were reminded of how coaching (and mentoring) had impacted Niki's life at the beginning of her sales career. She'd gone to work at a small, successful agency that specialized in real estate, insurance and other investment products. Although it was a small town and a small agency, competition was keen. She had little guidance from management and no training, yet expectations were high. Niki was floundering. She was on 100 percent commission, there was a quota and as a single mom she had no fallback position. She had to produce or starve.

One day, hoping to learn this woman's secret, she asked the most successful broker in the office to lunch and was brusquely turned down! "What for," Elsbeth replied. "I don't go to lunch unless it's to work!" Refusing to get discouraged, Niki persisted, and was finally rewarded with a yes, but only to coffee, not lunch.

That afternoon started a coaching relationship that altered Niki's sales career for the better. Elsbeth, a gruff, heavily accented Pennsylvania-Dutch German, gave sound advice and Niki modeled it for years to come. Over coffee, Elsbeth opened her wallet, reached in and took out a wrinkled $100 bill (and this was during the '70s when a $100 bill had some value). "This is my secret," said Elsbeth. "I carry this or another $100 bill always, on every appointment, even though I sometimes need it for groceries for me and the boys, and it's hard sometimes to keep from spending it," (Elsbeth, a widow, had four teenage sons).

"I don't understand," Niki said.

"Well, think," Elsbeth snapped, "if I have a $100 bill, I don't need the money from *that* sale. I won't compromise just for the commission or force something on a client that's not in his best interest. As long as I don't *need* the sale I can focus on what's best for my client."

Over the next year much conversation was held over coffee, and Niki learned the art and science of consultative selling. She went out on calls with Elsbeth, was critiqued by Elsbeth. She learned to tape her calls and play them back for critique. The day finally came when Niki was a consistent top producer, and more important, she had a $100 bill tucked into her wallet she did not "need."

Coaching has been used for years as an integral part of sports. Winning teams have winning coaches who call the shots, discipline, encourage and lead their teams to peak performance. Some coaching greats are household names, John Wooden, Bear

Bryant, Vince Lombardi, Lou Holtz, Bobby Knight, the list could go on.

Yet many of the same principles that sports coaches use to spur their sports teams to greater success can be used by parents to build better children and families, and by managers to develop people dedicated to giving their best and to being their best. Coaching builds better performance. In its simplest form, coaching is the art of giving constructive feedback, guidance and support on an individual basis to the members of any team.

Whether it is in sports, families or business, almost any one of us can thrive on good coaching. Our experience lends itself best to on-the-job business coaching so we'll confine our comments to this one area. We also believe coaching is critical to business success. The old management model of planning, organizing, staffing, directing and controlling is not nearly as successful as it once was, given today's work teams.

Employees today are less loyal than they've ever been—and with good cause. They expect more, demand more, want more information, are better educated and are more of a challenge than previous generations. The baby boomer knows his or her job will not lead to a gold watch and that instead it may lead to downsizing or early retirement. The Generation X'er wants ownership and empowerment and fun. He or she wants more time to devote to activities outside of work. The manager has his or her hands full and is expected to do more with fewer resources and people.

Coaching is the current buzzword in corporate America today. This has unfortunate consequences because it tends to make it into a fad, not something to be treated seriously. Coaching may have a tendency to be exploited by those who call themselves coaches or by managers who claim they coach, and yet truly do not understand what the real meaning and purpose of coaching is.

What is coaching? It's a skill, as well as an art, it's performance-related and capable of fostering breakthroughs and results. The dictionary defines the verb "coach" as: "to tutor, train, give hints to, prime with facts." This definition does not give it justice. Coaching can deliver spectacular results because of the relationship that grows between coach and student and the way they communicate. It builds a foundation of trust, mutual respect and support.

Coaching can unlock an individual's potential so they can maximize their own performance. It helps employees learn, stretch and grow. Coaching allows management to give constructive feedback, guidance and support to individual members of their team. A directive process, it allows managers to train and orient employees to the work environment and optimize their work performance. The coaching process allows expectations to be jointly set, action plans developed between manager and employee, and expected behavior nurtured to its best outcome. In addition, a mutual respect deepens as the relationship between manager and employee revolves around a bond of new trust and more open communication.

Coaching becomes even more necessary as companies restructure, change jobs, change peoples' titles and job descriptions and lay people off. The increasingly competitive environment in which companies function has put greater demands on managers who are now doing much of their own administrative work. Employees are expected to do more, work longer hours and yet often have less structure to their job. They're expected to know more about their present job and the work of others so they can "chip in when needed," and understand the new technology that makes it all possible. Managers today must lead through a common vision and support a team environment—that is, if they want results. Massive change, outsourcing, globalization, and the diverse demographics companies are faced with call for a new management model.

Coaching builds a more productive work environment and enhances the development of skills and performance to do the new work expected. A manager may want to use coaching:

1. *To improve substandard performance*—This coaching approach might be more directive, working with an employee to understand the standards to provide training and to set new expectations.

2 *To maintain standard performance*—The desired behavior is reinforced through rewards and strategic action plans. The purpose of this level of coaching is to motivate employees to come to work and do the job they're paid for, stay interested in and satisfied with their jobs as well as turn out satisfying work.

3. *To improve standard performance*—This is best used for those individuals who are meeting expectations. Its purpose is to develop individuals and help them exceed standard performance and build toward new skills and best practices.

In the restructured, reengineered, "right-sized." lean and mean organization, the old command and control management style must give way to a new improved management structure that supports open communication, listening, respect and an "I own my job" mentality.

The manager as coach works to:

- Build performance
- Instill confidence
- Enhance motivation
- Develop skills
- Clarify expectations
- Confront difficulties and conflicts
- Encourage flexibility

The manager as coach must use interpersonal skills to motivate and inspire and build relationships and teams committed to the company's vision.

To some degree managers are responsible for building the self-esteem and self-confidence of employees, training them so they perform optimally, and coaching and mentoring employees on their career path. Managers must confront behavior and performance that is not productive or that is below the employees' own standards, mentor them for best practices and create a learning organization that recognizes and rewards the performance needed.

Building on our intellectual capital is not an easy task. It is through coaching that managers build supportive, collaborative relationships. Coaching allows for interactions that provide the learning tools necessary for future growth. In this role as coach, managers maximize performance by taking on several coaching roles:

- *The Coach as Trainer:* Coaches assist their workers in developing technical knowledge. It is their job to recognize the gaps between what an employee needs to know and what he or she does know and to address those gaps immediately.
- *The Coach as Role Model:* Coaches model the behavior they expect. They walk their talk, are present, catch employees doing the job right and give them on-the-spot coaching.
- *The Coach as Confronter:* Coaches do not shirk a problem or ignore situations until they are too late to do anything about. Coaches identify the gaps between present and expected performance and build commitment to ongoing improvement. They are not afraid to communicate expectations and standards, set and stretch goals and challenge individuals who are already successful performers to attain even greater excellence. In this role, they strive to produce desired change without evoking lasting defensiveness.

- *The Coach as Mentor:* In this role, the manager serves as a mentor to help further an individual's career growth. They encourage risk-taking, thinking and stretching outside the box. As a mentor, a manager can help his or her employee with further opportunities that may advance a career. A savvy manager builds the individual's worth for the company by educating him or her on how the organization runs, its politics, how to network and how to handle crisis. A sharp and caring mentor can pave the way for new work opportunities for his mentee. It can be a win-win growth experience for both. Mentors teach and lead by example and "push" for greater results.

In the book, *Mentoring and Assessing,* the authors say, "Coaching is directly concerned with the immediate improvement of performance and development of skills by a form of tutoring and instruction. Mentoring is always one step removed and is concerned with the longer-term acquisition of skills in a developing career by a form of advising and counseling." There is no reason why a manager can't do a combination of both.

Yet to coach successfully we have to be willing to take an optimistic view of the hidden potential of our people. Managers must believe people have more potential than they presently exhibit. The manager must be trained to think of people in terms of their future potential. That potential may in fact be different from their present performance.

Coaching is much more than a canned technique that managers can turn off and on at will. It is not about rigid structures and a step-by-step way of dealing with all people the same way. It is about management that treats people differently based on the individual (as in Tony Alessandra's Platinum Rule). It is about a new way of thinking and being that demands a higher level of integrity and empathy and new ways of dealing with time.

Coaches help to figure out what people are good at and then they put them in situations where they can utilize those strengths. It's necessary to know, understand and appreciate both individual and team strengths and weaknesses, remembering that there are no perfect people. It means acting like coaches, *not* cops! People can and do appreciate and value our input if we provide a learning environment conducive to growth.

In the coaching environment we need some definition of what to do when our employees' motivation and skills are not what they should be in order to do their best. Depending on whether an employee is higher or lower on motivation and skills, we will coach differently. Our styles need to be flexible, depending on the circumstances and the individual being coached.

As a result, we:

- direct if both motivation and skill are low.
- inspire if motivation is low and skill is high.
- delegate if both motivation and skill are high.
- guide if motivation is high and skill is low.

Effective coaching can help guide people into better choices, more responsible behavior and more productive performance. Coaches working with employees, listening to their needs, asking good questions and providing good feedback can validate the growth process. Today's manager is a skilled communicator who *REAPS*™ the crop he grows through coaching by....

- **R**eviewing with the individual being coached the expected standards of performance and what behavior and goals are expected.
- **E**valuating the progress the individual has attained thus far.
- **A**nalyzing the game plan the individual had previously set and what was or was not achieved.
- **P**lanning for future growth and development.
- **S**olutions and action plans that will aid the individual in being more productive and meeting their and the company's goals.

Granted there are pitfalls and barriers to overcome in coaching. We may claim we've tried it before with no success; we might be too impatient and demand instant success; we may not set clearly defined and specific goals and action plans, or lack persistence, or fail to inspire the trust needed to make it work. We might even be apprehensive of the commitment and time needed to invest in coaching.

Good coaching is an art. It demands good listening, flexibility and empathy. Coaches are optimistic and empathetic. Coaches know that *all* people have value and it may just need to be brought out and polished. And good coaches don't take themselves too seriously!

What good coaches do is identify:

- the performance we'd like to see in an employee.
- how we will monitor that progress.
- the possible negative or positive effects we see in performance.
- what works best with this individual, what does not.
- what the objective of the coaching session is.
- how to provide opportunities to learn new skills, growth and challenges.

Coaching helps people see the link between their behavior and the expected results, in a safe environment. We can coach on the spot when we observe behavior that's working well. Wherever the coaching takes place, let people know the session has two primary objectives: to support and empower them to be increasingly successful and to enable them to be even more effective at producing the results they and you want. Help individuals see that they have a responsibility for the situation and that they can act in large or small ways toward solutions.

Not all coaching has to be long term like Niki and Elsbeth's. On the spot coaching may also have long term payoffs. Take our friend (and board member for the McCuistion television program and the Foundation for Responsible Television), Dr. Terry Flowers. Born on the south side of Chicago, Terry, his two sisters and three brothers were brought up by his widowed mom. Life was not easy, yet the family stuck together. Terry had great opportunities for education and he took advantage of them. Yet at college graduation time he was torn between getting his masters degree and being drafted by the Chicago Bears.

He was leaning toward the Bears the day he walked into his counselor's office to discuss both possibilities. After all, the Bears would have enabled him to make life easier for his family. He outlined his choices to the counselor. At the end of his discussion the counselor leaned back and said, "Terry, follow your heart, do what's right for you. Yet consider this, if you go with the Bears you'll have a chance at giving your family nice things, that is, *if* you make the team, and that's a real long shot. If you go on to more education you'll have a chance to help more than your family. You'll *have* a chance to help your people (Terry is African-American). You might be able to teach someday, and really make a difference to many people's future."

Terry chose to be a teacher, and today he is the headmaster of St. Philip's School in Dallas, where six percent of the children attending are on scholarships and live in the surrounding poor, crime-ridden neighborhood. He emphasizes values and goal-setting, which have allowed his kids to succeed long after they leave St. Philip's. And all because of a fifteen-minute coaching session more than twenty years ago.

Fundamentally, the success or failure of today's business depends on the leader's ability to coach, develop, empower, facilitate and reinforce its human infrastructure—its employees—to be accountable for achieving, expressing and producing their best at all times. James Kouzes and Barry Posner said in their book, *The Leadership Challenge*,

> Coaches don't wait until the season is over to let their players know how they are doing. The same should be true in your business. Coaching involves the on-the-job, day-by-day spending of time with your people, talking with them about your game strategies, and providing them feedback about their efforts and performance. And when the game is over, you get together with your players and analyze the results of your efforts. Where did we do well? Where do we need to improve our efforts? What will we have to do differently, better, or more of the next time?

We leave it up to you. Can one person make a difference? Coaches do every day.

A COACHING MODEL©1998 McCUISTION & ASSOC.

- Establish the purpose of the discussion and its importance.
- Discuss and clarify details about the situation.
- Mutually agree on what needs to be accomplished.
- Discuss the alternatives for achieving success.
- Seek agreement together on specific action(s) to be taken.
- Express confidence in the individual and set a date for evaluating.

3

THE POWER & MAGIC OF COACHING

Deborah Lindholm
888-303-COACH
619-454-0544
lindholmd@aol.com

Deborah Lindholm is a professional coach. She has spent more than twenty-five years in education, business and counseling settings assisting people in achieving their personal goals and dreams. Her international business experience is extensive. She is founder and executive director of the Foundation for Women, a nonprofit corporation that sponsors retreats for women for the exploration of mind, body and spirit in environments that foster personal enrichment. Deborah has a master's degree in education and counseling and is currently completing a Ph.D. program. She is actively involved in community affairs, most notably Rotary, hospice and child abuse prevention and participates on several boards.

"And what do you do?" is a question asked often in everyday conversations. My answer: I am a professional coach. I have spent more than twenty-five years in education, business and counseling settings helping people achieve their goals and dreams. I now have a business with a card that simply states what I do—Deborah Lindholm, Coach.

What is professional coaching? It is a profession bursting forth in support of all those with dreams yet to be fulfilled. It is about inspiring others to win. Professional coaches:

- assist individuals and businesses in focusing energy toward defined goals
- offer unconditional support, structure and feedback
- enhance clients' performances and achievements
- ask clients to do more than they would do on their own
- bring a winning spirit to clients

Note: Professional coaching was once a perk confined to high level executives, but now is available to (and is being used by) a variety of people in a multitude of circumstances.

A personal story explains how professional coaching came to be part of my life—and what I have been able to do because of coaching.

A GIANT LEAP OF FAITH

"Hi—I'm Deborah. I'd like to talk with you about jumping out of airplanes." I don't know where that came from—or why. I just knew. And I knew I couldn't do it alone.

HOW DID I GET TO THAT POINT IN MY LIFE?

I grew up in the era of girls' PE—not girls' sports. I was always tall for my age. I would have been a great basketball player or track participant. But the opportunities were not available. So I poured my energies into academic pursuits (and helped raise four younger sisters). I won a wager with my father as to who would complete a targeted college degree first; I finished a master's degree in education and then subsequent work in counseling. Sports and coaches were for others—mostly men.

One day a woman working with me asked if I would like to run a marathon. How far is that? I wondered but didn't have the courage to ask.

Kathryn and I connected immediately. Her warm special manner invited me to be open to the possibility. I had just accepted a mid-year transfer to a junior high school special education resource position. Kathryn came with the job; she was a bright spot in the chaos. *No coincidence.*

To her challenge I said "Why not?" We started running. The first run was from the mailbox on the corner to the ocean a few blocks away and back. Kathryn talked—I panted. She asked—I agreed. She believed—I trusted. We ran.

We ran and ran and ran—and slapped the mailbox on the corner in triumph after each run. We went from that first mile run to one a little farther—and then a little farther—until we were running miles and miles each afternoon. We went from supporting the most at-risk kids all day to supporting ourselves by putting on our shoes and running each afternoon.

We talked and processed and wondered and hoped— but mostly we ran under Kathryn's strong knowing and support. A marathon was possible for me. She held the space of believing in me and in that reality. She never faltered. She supported me through my early 10K races, which each took an hour and all my strength. How could I ever find more than four times that effort? Kathryn believed I could. I started to believe.

We ran more 10Ks; then we ran half-marathons. John and Ralph joined as part of "the team." They came for themselves and in support of me. *No coincidence.* Three of them already had run marathons—many marathons. But not me. We all ran.

Then it was time. We had done enough long after-work runs. I had come to know the streets and neighborhoods of San Diego in a very different way. I had finished a half-marathon with exuberance and even with something left. I was ready for the next step. And I had Kathryn—she believed in me.

The running group committed to running the Avenue of the Giants Marathon in the redwood trees north of San Francisco. It was known to be a beautiful run, but also known to be very difficult to obtain a running entry. Kathryn believed. We were all accepted. *No coincidence.*

We ran! Most importantly for me, I ran 26.2 miles one early morning. I had come to believe in me—that I could—because Kathryn had held that space for me for months. I could be part of an elite group of people. I could be a marathon runner.

I was in my early thirties when I completed that first marathon. The achievement was remarkable. Equally remarkable was that it was the first time in my life that I had experienced the power—and magic—of someone really, truly believing in me, supporting me to achieve; and offering me a space to step into. It was great!

Today, fifteen years later I am still a marathon runner. I have coached many others to reach the marathon dream. This has happened because I stepped into the space a coach first held for me with the implicit message: I could do it. I could do it well. I could succeed. I could be a winner.

Since then, I have run many marathons. And I have run more half-marathons than I can count. And I have run more miles than I would really like to know. Running is a core part of my life and of who I am. Thank you, Kathryn, for believing in me.

Her belief fostered my own belief in what I can do when I am in running shorts and shoes for many years now. I can accomplish anything with those props. In 1997, I ran the London Marathon—finishing within a minute of the time I had clocked so many years earlier in the redwoods. It does not matter to me how many completion certificates I have vis-a-vis someone else; what my time is versus someone else's or what my running goals are versus someone else. What *does* matter is that I continually keep the focus on me and strive to do my personal best—in running and in all aspects of my life.

How do I function without the running props? The sense of strength and confidence I have gained from running has greatly enhanced my life. I have not always, however, been able to carry that strength with me. I have been unable to find it in places where I really wanted it: at the observation deck at the Eiffel Tower, on the cable car from Singapore to Sentosa Island; on a journey inside the great pyramids of Egypt; when standing in front of an unfamiliar audience. I have lost it when I really wanted to pull it forth—but couldn't find it.

Only I have known this to be my truth. And what I knew was important. Others knew I had excelled in all areas where I decided to focus my attention—whether in education, business, philanthropic causes, or in my commitments to others. Yet I knew there was more toward which I should reach.

Unexpectedly in 1997, a situation presented itself involving a chance to look at my strength and confidence, as well as my fear. I heard a speaker at a professional coaching conference comment on how it is human nature to seek comfort and avoid pain; that growth and accomplishment result from stretching, from resisting the desire to seek comfort.

As a Ph.D. candidate in psychology, I had heard what this speaker had to say many times and knew it to be the truth. He shared his personal story—which included a tremendous fear of heights and what he had done to overcome it. He had taken up the sport of skydiving. What was important for me is that his presentation triggered awareness in me. *No coincidence.* I knew I was once again challenged and ready to stretch my abilities.

It has been said that *when the pupil is ready the teacher will appear.* At the end of the keynote speech, I knew that I was going to jump out of an airplane. I could think of nothing more dramatic or challenging—or more frightening. I committed. I knew I could do it. I knew I would do it. I also knew I would not do it alone.

In response to my introduction to him, the presenter asked me to give him a business card with "sky dive" on the back. I pulled a card from my purse. I watched my hand write "sky dive." I was committed. I handed the card to him.

I didn't wait for the presenter to contact me after the conference. I called him. I was going to achieve this goal. I needed a coach.

Weeks passed—much to my surprise—before a date could be scheduled. I had always been able to "hurry, fix it, make it better, get it done." Now I was being asked to find patience and to trust. Weather, schedules, broken camera: were these all signs that I was not supposed to jump? The questioning came for only moments. I knew I was going to jump—the only real question was when.

The time of anticipation was an integral and necessary part of my process. This jump was about so much more than confronting discomfort with heights and fear. It was about trust and timing and letting go. It was also about determination—unwavering determination despite the delays.

It has been said that life expands in relation to one's courage. I also know from years of working with hospice patients and their families that the regrets at the end of life are not for things done, but rather for things not done. This opportunity to jump from an airplane—to make a great leap in my life—was presenting itself to me at what I considered the midpoint of my life. I was determined to have the second half be different from the first. I did not want to collect any more regrets.

I had the courage. I had the commitment. I had the coach. And I had a small rock that said, "Trust God."

The coaching process challenged me to think big, to realize my greatness, to commit to a state of discomfort. Coach Bob held a space representing success and achievement for me. He asked me to step into that space—just as Kathryn had done so many years previously.

As the scheduled day approached, I became more contemplative. What did I want to let go of besides fear? There was more. A list of eleven things came into being. I wrote the list the night before the jump. I was determined to let go of all of them.

After days of wind and rain and cold, the day dawned beautiful and sunny and clear. *No coincidence.* I was full of gratitude—for the weather, the day, the courage, the commitment and for the coach. If I were to falter, I knew he would support me. I was ready.

I drove north on Interstate 15 to Perris, California. As I was exiting the freeway and feeling unsure of how to get to the airport, I saw a woman walking down the road with a parachute. I stopped and offered her a ride. She was Cathy from Michigan. She inquired about my reason for coming to Perris and then expressed excitement about my jump. How many had she done? I asked. "Oh, over 1100—I jump all over the world," she said. 1100!! I certainly could do one! Cathy was a sign of encouragement and boosted my confidence. *No coincidence.*

I walked to the skydiving school with calm contemplation, clutching my rock. Since I had made this commitment, I had heard more skydiving stories than I ever thought possible. "Oh yes, my sons have done that!" "I know a family that does that often." "Did you hear about the lost skydivers over..." But my jump was not about anyone else or any other's experience. It was about me.

I was to do all the necessary paperwork and then meet up with Bob. He not only would be my coach, but would also film the jump. I watched a video that explained the dangers of what I was to do and the impossibility of legal recourse if something were to go wrong. I signed the multi-page release form. I was ready.

Just after 2 p.m. I was called to get into a jumpsuit. I wanted a blue one. I held my rock. As I was stepping into the suit, my jump-master Vinny arrived—with a smile and a confidence that enveloped me. *No coincidence.* He looked me straight in the eyes and asked "Are you ready to go have some fun?" I was ready.

Vinny never left my side from that first moment. He held a space for me that was so special. Not only would I jump, I would jump well.

At 12,500 feet I jumped. I let go of my small paper with the eleven big things. I jumped into a space that a coach and a jump-master held for me. I succeeded! I free-fell to 5,000 feet, then pulled the ripcord. The chute opened. I hovered nearly a mile over the earth—over the snow-capped mountains, Lake Elsinore, the freeway I had been on just hours earlier, the ocean in the distance, and the small spot that was the Perris Airport. I glided to earth slowly, savoring the unbelievableness of it all.

I landed with assuredness—just as the whole process had been for me. *No coincidence.* I said "Thank you God, Thank you Vinny, Thank you Bob," and then used a one-word vocabulary for the rest of the day—"Unbelievable!"

I hadn't sought comfort. I'd gone the other direction—through the fear to the greatest spot imaginable. It was confirmed again for me. There is power—and magic—in coaching.

THE EMERGENCE OF PROFESSIONAL COACHING

When the greatest names in sports are mentioned, Deborah Lindholm is not among them. Muhammad Ali, Nadia Comaneci, Martina Navratilova, Michael Jordan are listed. They personify years of dedication and hard work, incredible talent, unparalleled success. In addition, these supreme athletes have something else in common—a coach who offered them unwavering support, continually asked for more and who held a space of greatness for their students.

The dictionary confirms the connection of coach to sports. It defines a coach as "a person who trains athletes or athletic teams." That definition is now expanding. The Professional & Personal Coaches Association defines coaching as "an ongoing relationship that focuses on clients taking action toward the realization of their visions, goals and desires." This definition certainly fits marathon running as well as jumping out of an airplane. But it also fits building a business or starting a foundation—or any other vision, goal or desire.

Professional coaching takes the principles of athletic coaching and adds a deep respect for the individual's inner knowing. It is a process of inquiry that leads to awareness and then action. Consultants have the right answers; professional coaches have the right questions.

A key to professional coaching is to hold the client's agenda. The client has a vision, goal or desire. Powerful questions are posed by the coach to elicit awareness—and then followed by action. What does a successful business look like to you? When can you complete the marketing plan? Where do you need to say no? Who are the key players in the organization regardless of title? How much effort are you willing to commit to this? The client decides what to do.

The goal of a professional coaching relationship is to maximize human potential and at the same time maintain life balance. There are many aspects to a life: profession, finances, physical well-being, primary relationship/family, other relationships, spirituality, personal development, physical surroundings, rest and relaxation, among others. All areas need attention if balance is to be maintained.

As the coaching process develops, the client leads the agenda and the coach offers support, structure and feedback. Part of the support is to build in responsibility. The coach makes direct requests of the client; for example, "I have a request: Will you write the memo by Friday and fax me a copy?" It is then up to the client to accept the request, say no to it or alter it in some way to make it acceptable.

Professional coaching is an empowerment process. The client is in charge and commits and then takes action. How different this is from the usual experience in a traditional "tell" instead of "ask" management format: do this, this way, by this date. The old exterior imposition model is replaced in the coaching process by an internal decision-making, personal-ownership model.

The professional coaching relationship is about integrity. When I said "Yes" to Kathryn and when I said "Yes" to Bob, I knew I would run a marathon and I knew I would jump from an airplane. Making these commitments aloud to another human being made them real for me. I had pledged my word. And I was committed to a relationship. Not only would I accomplish these tasks for me, but I would accomplish them with a sense of gratitude for the support and belief in me by another.

One of my clients shared the following missive with me. It speaks to the power and magic of the coaching process.

TO: My Coach

FROM: The Client Who Is Creating Today!

Where can I go and receive the following:

- Unconditional support
- Someone who always holds the big picture for me
- Someone who points out my achievements and, no matter how small they are, she says they are big!
- Someone with whom I can plan my life
- Someone who provides clarity around what my truth is
- Someone who can play with my gremlins (self-doubts) and have fun at the same time
- Someone who offers spiritual, emotional, physical and intellectual feedback and new perspectives
- Someone I can always count on no matter where my head is
- Someone who will ask me to stretch because he or she knows I can and that it would support my desires and dreams
- Someone who is fun on the phone—really!
- Someone in the world who is out there thinking about me and who believes that I have special gifts to offer

Here are a few reasons I choose to have a coach...I choose to have you as my coach! I know there are many others too!

APPLICATIONS OF PROFESSIONAL COACHING

A professional coaching colleague once stated, "If I'd had a coach as a young professional, I wouldn't be a late-bloomer."

Professional coaching is now an integral part of numerous situations. Coaches are helping corporations improve the bottom line. Coaches are supporting entrepreneurs in growing businesses. Coaches are assisting students in schools—in one case, taking payment in pictures and poetry. Coaches are encouraging creative expression. Coaches are supporting the unique brilliance that is in each being.

I have been and am continually liberated from my fears as a result of the talented and committed coaches in my life. I strive to give that gift of liberation to others in my work and in my being.

I have been blessed to be part of many special stories of winning. Larry's story is a very special one. We met one Thursday afternoon. I had been volunteering my time with patients and families at San Diego Hospice for many years. I entered his room to see if he had finished lunch. I introduced myself and we shook hands.

I was immediately struck by his warmth and by his welcoming manner, considering his circumstances. Larry looked me directly in the eye as we spoke. He noticed my Rotary pin and asked about my club.

I learned that he was an attorney, a judge, the father of two young boys, and that yoga had been part of his life. A few weeks earlier he had gone to the doctor complaining of a sore back. He thought he had pulled a muscle while doing yoga. The doctor could find nothing wrong and sent him home. The pain persisted and intensified. After weeks more of pain, an MRI medical procedure was ordered. The pain was from cancer—cancer that had spread throughout his body. There was no treatment. Larry was referred to San Diego Hospice.

One of Larry's first questions to me was, "What do you do when you are not at Hospice?" My response to this question tends to vary with the circumstances. To say I'm a professional coach most often brings an inquisitive look and an inquiry of "Sports?" At times I respond with a past title—I am a counselor. But there was no hesitation on my part in responding to Larry's question. "I am a professional coach," I said.

"Oh that's great! I've worked with one for many years," he said. *No coincidence.* Another coaching connection had happened for me.

Not everyone is a candidate for coaching. Coaching is for those who want to grow and stretch—and realize they will achieve more with support. Larry was ready to grow and stretch through this last part of this journey.

I was available. I offered unconditional support. I held Larry's agenda. I gave feedback when asked. I shared when appropriate. I listened. I was totally present for him.

In the following weeks, Larry's physical world constricted as more and more bodily functions ceased operation. At the same time, his mental and spiritual world grew. He read and questioned and listened to tapes and processed what he had learned. He stepped to the plate and used each of his moments. He shared his insights and wishes—and his increasing peace.

Connected to family and special friends, Larry died just eight weeks after his diagnosis. His is a very special story of winning—of taking what life presents and growing with it, not shrinking from it. His is a story of commitment and courage, not fear. His is a story of joining with others to enhance his experience, and theirs. His is a story of inspiring others to win.

߄

EVERYONE NEEDS A COACH!

Todd Duncan
619-551-0905
joolzsg@aol.com

Todd Duncan believes that in order to achieve excellence in life and in business, you need the right purpose, the right attitude and the right skills backed by the right relationships. *Then you will receive the power to be your best.* Todd's presentations are based on his successful experience in retail and wholesale lending, banking, finance and real estate. Participants in his programs report that they have gained control of their lives, maximized their personal productivity and enhanced their commitments to important relationships and customers.

Man is the only animal that laughs and weeps, for he is the only animal that is struck with the difference between what things are and what they ought to be.

—William Hazlitt

Never try to be better than someone else but never cease being the best you can be.

—Coach John Wooden

Olympic Gold Medalist Michael Johnson has one! One of the greatest Olympians in history, Bonnie Blair has one. The winners of the Ironman Triathalon, Thomas Hellriegel and Heather Fuhr, have one. Perhaps the greatest basketball player who has ever lived, Michael Jordan, has one! The first and youngest player on the PGA Tour to ever win more than $2 million in one year, Tiger Woods, has one! Leaders of some of the greatest companies on earth have them. And increasingly, thousands of individuals each year are seeking coaching relationships to help them gain and maintain a more productive and meaningful life. Behind every great accomplishment there stand two people—the person who teaches and the person who executes. Perhaps it's time that you consider the benefits of a coach!

WHAT IS A COACH?

In February 1988 while attending a Tom Hopkins seminar, I learned the lesson of the value of this life. Early in the morning, Tom said, "There are not many things you need to have a more productive and meaningful life. In fact, each and every one of you embody the ingredients for success. But more important, *you must think like a winner and you must have a coach.*"

He then began to ask some of the most powerful questions I have ever heard:

- How valuable is your life to you?
- How important is the time that your life gives to you?
- What has more value, this building you are seated in or your life?
- How long do you think it took to "plan" this building?
- Then what is your conclusion?

How Valuable Is Your Life To You?

How would you have responded to these questions? Here were my answers: How important is the time that your life gives to you? The answer, obviously, is *Very.*

What has more value, this building you are seated in or your life? *My life!*

How long do you think it took to "plan" this building? *Eighteen months.*

Then what is your conclusion? *That if my life is more important than this building, why have I not spent eighteen months planning it? Why have I not even spent eighteen days? Or eighteen hours?*

I was deeply affected—by what happened that morning and it caused me to act. First, the statement, "You must think like a winner" and second, the statement, "You must have a coach." These, of course, are the central tenets of what makes every Olympian great—they think like winners and they hire or otherwise engage others to help them become winners—personally and professionally.

Halfway through his seminar, I approached Mr. Hopkins and mentioned to him that I wanted to be a speaker, a thought that I had been pondering for years, but now with "Olympic thinking" clearly in place, I was ready to act. I asked him if he could help. He said, "See me after the seminar and I'll talk with you.

When it became my turn, I approached Mr. Hopkins and before saying a word, he asked, "So you want to be a speaker?" I barely began to nod my head affirmatively when he asked the second question, "When will you be one?"

He said, "Until you decide when you are going to be one, you will never begin doing the things that lead to your becoming one." He asked again, "So, when will you be one?" I thought quickly and said, "July 6, 1988." He said, "Take your planner out and write that date down. And, if I don't hear from you by that date, I will call you and ask you why you have not held to the commitment you have just made to yourself."

In that moment, I went from thinking about being a speaker to being committed to becoming one. In the course of one day, Tom Hopkins had become my mentor—someone I wanted to be like; my model, someone who could show me how; and my motivator, someone who could get me to act. I had found my first coach!

Several months went by as I continued to think of my commitment. About two weeks before July 6, I called Mr. Hopkins and, as expected, he was not in. Two days later he returned my call from Atlanta's Hartsfield Airport and spent forty-five minutes with me on the phone, coaching me on how to become a professional speaker. He told me what to do to market myself, he told me what to do to promote myself, he told me how to speak in order to become highly sought after, and he told me to never ever give up—the Olympic mindset!

At that end of that conversation, he said, "If you ever need me, feel free to call and I will help you." This is a hallmark character trait of successful coaches—they give because someone once did the same for them—this is the Law of Reciprocity.

FIVE CHARACTER TRAITS OF WINNING COACHES

In his relationship with me, Tom Hopkins demonstrated the five character traits of winning coaches. Consider these as you seek a coach and perhaps again as you become one:

- He let me tell him what I wanted to do (my goals).
- He let me tell him when I was going to do it (my deadline).
- He told me the consequence of not doing it (my motivation).
- He taught me how to do what I wanted to do (my model).
- He became available to me and evaluated my progress (my mentor and accountability partner).

Using what Mr. Hopkins taught me, I have built a successful speaking and writing business, making a difference in tens of thousands of people's lives every year. I owe my success to my desire and Tom's coaching.

HOW DO YOU FIND YOUR MENTOR/COACH?

John Maxwell, president and CEO of InJoy Ministries in Atlanta offers the following key question in selecting a Mentor/Coach: "Do I want to be like this person?" A way to determine that is by using the ABC's of selecting a mentor coach:

- Attitude—Can this person teach me how to think right?
- Belief—Does this person believe in me?
- Character—Is this a life worth following?
- Development—Can this person develop me?

- Experience—Does this person have a wide range of experiences?
- Fruitfulness—Has there been "success" in his/her life?
- Growth—Is this person still growing?

The point of selecting a mentor/coach is to improve. No matter what area of your life that you desire to change or would seek coaching for, all coaching arrives at the point of helping you discover and implement a "map" that has a high probability of getting you from where you are to where you want to go.

LESSONS FROM MY COACHES

No one makes it to the top by himself or herself. Over the last ten years, I have had several coaching relationships. I have had the pleasure of learning from and being coached by best-selling author and motivational speaker, Zig Ziglar. The president of the National Speakers Association, Glenna Salsbury, has been my business coach for the last eight years. Since the age of 15, Bob Shank, the President and CEO of Priority Living has been my spiritual and life coach.

Here are the lessons they taught me:

LESSON #1: ALL SUCCESS MUST HAVE A FIRM FOUNDATION

What is my purpose and why am I here?

All winners have a purpose and know the answer to the question, "Why am I here?" As you identify what your purpose is, you will find a new power of discipline and commitment. You will begin to reprioritize the commitments with which you approach your work, your relationships, your money, your body, and other aspects of your life.

My friend Bill Bachrach, author of *Values-Based Selling*, suggests you ask the question of yourself this way: The following is an excerpt from Bill's video, "The Values Conversation"— *What's important about success to me?*

Bill Bachrach: Todd, what's important about success to you?

Todd Duncan: One of the reasons I do what I do, Bill, is to earn a good living.

BB: Earning a good living is important to a lot of people for a lot of different reasons, Todd. Why is earning a good living important to you?

TD: If my earnings are good, it gives me freedom. The better they get, the less I have to work.

BB: Freedom is a good thing. Having more of it is important. Todd, tell me, why is freedom important to you?

TD: It gives me the chance to spend more time with my family and also provides an opportunity to do some speeches for Christian groups.

BB: I really appreciate the nature of what you want to do with your freedom. Out of curiosity, what's important about spending time with your family and speaking for Christian groups to you?

TD: It gives me a feeling of really making a difference.

BB: Is anything more important to you than making a difference.

TD: No

You can see by this dialog that my purpose is to make a difference. In discovering your own purpose, you must ask yourself similar questions. Becoming clear gives you added depth, direction, commitment and power in your daily life and forms the foundation from which everything develops.

LESSON #2: BEING AWARE OF WHAT YOU VALUE LEADS TO CLEARER VISION

What's important to me?

Once purpose is defined, it then can be applied to all the key areas of importance in your life. Some of the questions my coaches taught me to use to foster those thoughts are:

What do I value most in life?

What areas of my life that are important to me are not getting the attention they need?

What areas do I sense I need to move closer to in order to add fulfillment to my life?

What have I valued in the past that I no longer value and need to de-emphasize?

What gives others pleasure that I need to do more of?

A lifestyle that is focused on what you value is the second step for achieving a more productive and meaningful life. There is no other method that I have ever found to be effective in all of my years observing and coaching people to higher levels of performance than this crucial step.

As you explore each of these value areas, you will then be able to merge your purpose into an action plan. For example, I can now ask, "How can I make a difference in my relationship with my wife?" Or "How can I make a bigger difference in the lives of my children?" Or "How can I make a bigger difference with my money?" Or "What can I do with my body so that it is at peak performance in order that I can make a difference longer in other people's lives?" This is the power of living congruently with what you value.

The Elicitation Process:

What's important to me?

To clarify what you value is to answer as many times as you can the question, "What's important about life to me?"

Here are some sample answers:

- Family
- Financial security
- Health
- Personal development
- Intellectual growth
- Giving to others
- Integrity
- Spiritual vitality and my relationship with God
- Professional success

Once you have five to eight value areas, determine their order of importance and work on the most important ones first. This gives you momentum that feeds commitment.

Lesson #3: Without A Clear Vision, It's Easy to Go Off Course

What is my vision and where am I going?

Walt Disney once said, "If you can dream it, you can do it." The important thing in life is to be able to sacrifice what and where you are for what you could become and where you could be. All movement toward anything requires first knowing what that thing is.

You have asked the question, "What's important to me?" Now you must decide, based on the areas you have listed, where you want to be within each of those areas.

At the core is the discovery of what you want to be, have, or do, in the five to eight value areas of your life, and in what time frame you want to be, have, or do them. These time frames are "windows." The metaphor is simple—to see through to the possibilities of what is outside, you must be on the inside, looking out—the clearer the window, the better the picture!" I would suggest that these "windows" as long-term thoughts represent time frames of years.

As you develop a vision for each of the main value areas that you have determined, support them with a Clarifying Vision Statement. This serves as the centering mechanism, which on a daily, weekly, monthly and quarterly basis gives you the direction, focus and motivation to stay your course, to be committed. You now make lifestyle decisions based on these value areas. Here are two examples of Clarifying Vision Statements (CVS) that my coaches have helped me develop for two of the areas in my life I value.

1. Value: Spiritual vitality and my relationship with God.

CVS: My life is devoted to energizing people's passion and commitment to Christ and through active teaching and sharing, build His kingdom and make a difference, eternally.

2. Value: Health

CVS: My life is vibrant! I focus on the body and its fine tuning so that I may effectively enjoy an energy-rich life and experience the power to go the distance. By preserving my "temple" I fulfill my other values more consistently.

LESSON #4: A CLEAR MISSION KEEPS YOU ON COURSE
What are my shorter term goals in this value area?

LESSON #5: TO ARRIVE AT WHERE YOU WANT TO BE, YOU MUST CONSISTENTLY DO THE RIGHT THINGS
What will I do today to fulfill this value area?

Action produces results—the right actions produce the right results. And actions are more certain to occur if they are tied to your Clarifying Vision Statements. These actions or missions are short term. They take your "windows" which are five to ten years and break them into shorter "missions" that assist you in fulfilling your larger vision. With that determined, you then go to the short-term actions, which may be as frequently as daily. Precisely how often will be determined by you as you see the power of this model in action. Here's an example from my model as introduced to you. Watch carefully the difference between the mission (Lesson #4) and the daily activities (Lesson #5).

1. Value: Spiritual vitality and my relationship with God

    Mission: I am an evangelist, bringing my faith into my work and will write five Christian books by the age of 55, speak at least twenty times a year for Christian conferences, and actively help my local church in their educational needs.

    Daily Activities:

    - Study the Bible every day, selecting, cataloging, and storing verses that will have application to my works.
    - Read at least one other Christian book per month.
    - to further my knowledge.
    - Build and fill folders with research on the twenty main topics of interest that will fill my books.
    - Have an active prayer life each day seeking and following God's will for my life.

2. Value: Health

    Mission: I have a lifestyle that supports this vision, which includes maintaining a weight of 200 pounds, a cholesterol level of less than 160, and the proper workout and maintenance programs to maintain this outcome.

    Daily Activities:

    - Work out at least three times each week for at least thirty minutes while getting my heart rate to at least 130 beats per minute.
    - Avoid high fat foods that will deplete my energy and alter my mission.
    - Avoid fluids that diminish my clarity.

Every great Olympian follows these lessons. Your life will become more productive and your results will be more meaningful if you follow this model. Here is the application of this principle, stated by Henry David Thoreau:

> If one advances confidently in the direction of his dreams and endeavors to live the life he has imagined, he will meet with success unexpected in common hours. He will pass an invisible boundary; new universal and more liberal laws will begin to establish themselves around and within him; and he will live with the licenses of a higher order of being.

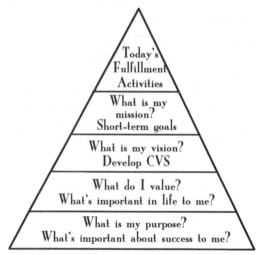

Today's
Fulfillment
Activities
What is my
mission?
Short-term goals
What is my vision?
Develop CVS
What do I value?
What's important in life to me?
What is my purpose?
What's important about success to me?

THE PYRAMID

Develop the habit of spending fifteen minutes every morning or the evening before reviewing your pyramid, starting at the bottom and working your way up to the top. Become intentional about scheduling the activities for every value area so that you achieve maximum productivity and meaningfulness in your life.

The Pyramid is your "map" to success. You will have both good days and bad days. There are days in which you will forget to review your "map" and you will go off course. There are other days when you will be so tuned-in you will be unstoppable. The key is that no matter which day you have, stay focused on the "map." Whenever you are lost, it will bring you home. Share your Pyramid with your Mentor/Coach so that he or she can help you stay focused on getting the most important things done.

FINAL LESSONS FROM "THE COACH"—JOHN WOODEN

- Be true to yourself
- Help others
- Make each day your masterpiece
- Feast every day from good books, especially the Bible
- Build a shelter against a rainy day
- Make friendship a fine art
- Give thanks for your blessings
- Pray for guidance every day

Your past does not equal your future—for it can be anything you decide you want it to be—today. Peace of mind in life and in business comes from knowing you have done your best. *Decide this moment to find a coach and you will capture the power to be your best!* This life is a race worth running with all of your might. At the finish line is the greatest reward you could ever receive, a life fulfilled.

℘

5

SEVEN SIMPLE STEPS TO FINDING A MENTOR

James Melton, Ph.D.
760 323-4204
info@4speakers.com
www.4speakers.com

James E. Melton, Ph.D. is one of America's outstanding platform artists. His enthusiasm inspires people to take action. Best-known as a motivator and humanistic futurist, he rose to prominence through his best-selling books and public television series, "Reaching New Heights of Excellence." His rich and varied background embodies an educated blend of experience that he has shared with Fortune 500 companies worldwide.

He is also the founder and president of The Agency for Speakers and Entertainers, a firm with twenty-five years in the professional speaking business that can locate and secure the services of any speaker or entertainer. *The New York Times* has recommended The Agency as a premier web site for meeting planners. His video-based training system is utilized internationally. Jim also delivers his message in French, when appropriate. He holds a Ph.D. in management.

The number seven is the number of completion. You see it repeatedly in nature—the seven colors of the rainbow, the seven precious gems, the seven deadly sins, the seven wonders of the world, to name only a few. This same number can also be applied during the process of finding a mentor. If you follow seven simple steps, you will be able to find the ideal person to assist you in realizing your goals.

1. CHOOSE YOUR RELATIONSHIPS WISELY

Choosing our friends and associates wisely is a critical factor for advancement in our personal lives, in business, and in community affairs. One of the first steps to self-enhancement and opening new doors is choosing your relationships wisely. There are people who enrich our lives and can benefit our present situation by their presence. These are action people, doers, open-minded people. When asked for an opinion, they tend to cast a positive light on the subject, continually seeking ways to encourage individuals to reach their dreams. Negative associations have caused many aspiring people to be passed over in consideration for an opportunity, a raise, or a promotion. These are people who rob us of our time, energy, and reputation.

Whom would you consider a competent person to seek advice? Think of someone who has achieved excellence in a field consistent with yours. Cultivating relationships with experienced individuals who can advise and guide you in a time of need, or simply offer insights based on their experience, is a priceless asset.

You might ask yourself, who was Einstein's teacher? Who inspired Bach? To whom does the president approach for counsel? For myself, Dr. James Ross was one of the greatest instruments in helping me lift my life to the next level. We met by chance at a talk I was presenting for Rotary. As a sensitive, academically wise individual, Jim Ross was instrumental in prompting me to extend my education. He encouraged me to break the patterns of my past and build a new vision for my future. Yes, mentors exist at all levels.

2. Don't Overlook Important Aspects of the Process

Let's take a look at some of the most often overlooked aspects of making a meaningful connection in a mentor relationship. These ideas will be helpful if you are going to be an example for others, or if you are looking toward another for inspiration and encouragement.

One of the elements that made my personal transition a reality was the result of something I had never seen before—even though it would have been quite evident had it been pointed out to me as I am about to do for you now. One overlooked aspect of finding a mentor is without usually realizing it, people generally tend to see in others qualities that lie deeply within themselves. Let's look briefly at admirable traits. You might see someone who is experiencing a healthy relationship, a prosperous business or a charismatic personality and say that you will never be able to receive such rewards from your efforts. Often the reason for the rejection and inability to identify with the attributes of others is we tend to look up to particular individuals as being unreachable. For instance, more times than not we place celebrities, notable politicians and sports figures in a category beyond the norm. Granted, these people have worked hard and most deserve their just rewards. But to place their stature beyond your reach is to discount your own abilities. This is why it is so important to realize that if we do admire a trait or quality of another, that very trait or quality also lies in us.

In the past, I would see or hear people that I thought had qualities I did not have and could not possess. Now I know differently. When I saw Dr. Wayne Dyer, author of *Your Erroneous Zones*, present his material in an eloquent manner, I admired him for his ability to convey a wealth of information and concrete examples. I also admired him for his obvious confidence to deliver his material in a manner that connected with every person in his audience. His delivery to the audience that evening was one of compassion, humor, and enthusiasm and contained a compelling message to move into action. The realization came to me that deep within myself I inherently possessed those same talents. Although my level of skill had not yet reached his, I did feel that my interest was strong enough to build myself to the point where I could create a financially profitable and rewarding lifestyle as a professional speaker and author. It was but only a few weeks later that I had tackled the task of writing my first book.

Another overlooked aspect of choosing a mentor would be a person's attitude. All you need to do is to follow someone around for a day or so and his or her results will tell all about that person's attitude of mind. You see, the results in our lives tend to directly reflect our thinking process. I've heard people say time and time again, "I've got a positive attitude, but I just have lousy results." That is surely not the case. A positive attitude produces positive results, and a negative attitude produces negative results.

I bring this up because if you are going to intentionally seek out a mentor, you will want to constructively take charge of your thinking and actions to attract to you the highest level of support possible. To do this successfully, practice is important. If you are new to the game of directing your thoughts, if you have formed some "bad" thinking habits. Fear not—they can be redirected. All habits are pieces of behavior built up over a period of time, and behavior can be changed moment by moment with directed conscious thoughts. But like playing the piano or learning a new language, it takes practice and certainly a desire to do it.

3. ASSOCIATE WITH PEOPLE YOU ADMIRE

Insights for personal growth may be gained by associating with people you admire. Consider their comments, activities and interests in order to learn from them and apply them. It goes without saying that if you want to speak French, it would be best to associate with people who are fluent in the French language. Along the same line, if you want to gain insights into profitable investments, your associations would lean strongly toward those who are wise investors.

My own experience with this approach occurred several years back when I attended a lecture by Wayne Dyer. Let me share with you how we became acquainted. Actually, I was in a position to ask him in for a lecture. I had just finished reading one of his latest books at that time. The book espoused self-actualization techniques. Risk-taking was one of them. Since I had never had the opportunity to hear him speak and wanted to, I thought I would take the risk. So, I phoned him directly. To my surprise, he answered the phone.

I said, "Wayne, this is Jim."

He said, "Jim, I don't know you, do I?"

I said, "No, but you will. I just finished reading one of the more enlightening books I have ever read, it's called *Your Erroneous Zones.*"

He said, "I wrote that."

I said, "I know—that's why I'm calling you. Would you consider coming to Denver to present a talk on the ideas you expressed in your book?" I was not surprised when he agreed.

What transpired over the next several months was, for me, the beginning of a mentorship that changed my life. By purposeful selection of someone whom I admired and by applying that person's suggestions, I was able to lift myself out of financial depression and relationship decline and elevate my personal world to a new height that I had not dreamed possible.

4. CONSCIOUSLY OBSERVE TRAITS OF OTHERS

To be more effective in your mentor selection process, observation of others is a major key. How do you define those people for whom you may wish to associate? Close observation of friends, loved ones, and colleagues will provide a real picture of your own thinking. So you need to become more conscious of how you go about selecting people with whom you would like to form relationships. Ask yourself what you see in others. You may relate quite well with one of your co-workers, but others in the office may find that particular individual difficult to deal with. Why do you suppose that is? What is it that causes an individual to be liked by some people and disliked by others? My belief is that the general tendency is to attract people who think in a similar fashion. This is why people with a similar religion, heritage and environment have such bonding strength.

Conversely, you may notice undesirable traits in people with whom you associate. This does not necessarily mean you possess the same traits. Be conscious of how you react when you are with this person. Do you observe their attitudes, actions, and opinions logically or do you get caught up in the emotions of your resistance? There is a distinct difference between observation and opposition, in other words, between acknowledgment and resistance. When a quality in another is strongly resisted, more likely than not that same quality exists within the person resisting. The person should look deeply within to better understand the nature of the resistance. Any person who desires positive change must not resist or suppress any negative trait, for by doing so, the individual is only masking an area requiring attention.

5. VIEW YOURSELF AS THE PERSON YOU WANT TO BE

Think about it. You are not so much the result of what you do, as you are the result of who you think you are. The mere fact that you have not yet realized how to express your talents is our major point of discussion here. The word "discover," simply means to uncover what has always been there.

When my good friend Archie Ulm came to town to present a special musical performance, I appreciated once again what a fantastic musician he was—truly a wizard at the keyboard. He could pull sounds out of that synthesizer like you have never heard before. There were about a thousand people in the grand ballroom of the hotel that day, and Archie performed with such artistry and mastery of his instrument that it brought chills to my spine. After the program, many people approached me to comment on the quality of Archie's music. I remember one person in particular who came up to me and said that he thought Archie was terrific and wished he had talent like that. He commented that he thought Archie was "a natural born musician." He continued saying that he wished he had talent like that. I told him that if he had spent as much time and effort, and had as much love and enthusiasm as Archie had for his music—practicing three to five hours a day for the past twenty years, he too would be able to do play like that. No, Archie is not "a natural born musician."

You see, the person was looking to Archie as one who possessed extraordinary musical gifts without effort. This was not the case. Archie saw himself as a talented musician and worked hard to become one. Any person longing for a talent needs to move into action. By thinking of yourself as possessing a talent, you will position yourself more effectively to express that talent.

6. PAY HEED TO CRITICISM

In a mentor relationship every individual should pay careful heed to any critical comments, suggestions, or hints that others may give about their behavior. Often others can see your personality in a way that you may not be able to see yourself. Not often will you be able to receive temperate, well-considered and explicit criticism from a friend. If, by good fortune, such criticism is offered, accept it as a valuable gift. As with any such gift, it should be thought over with the utmost care and on a deeper level, taken to heart, even if, on reflection, it cannot be wholly agreed upon.

Constructive critique can be found in any successful endeavor, such as sports, music, writing, or performing. Think about how much better an athlete can perform by having a coach critique his or her performance. Imagine Luciano Pavarotti without guidance of the conductor to intertwine his gift with that of the orchestra. Shouldn't every writer have an editor? And what choreographed ballet would not be enhanced by an outside expert opinion?

7. CONSIDER AN OUTSIDE SOURCE

You might think that advice is best offered by someone who exerts a strong influence over you, such as a family member. Although the part portrayed by a business manager, a spouse, a parent or a friend may be instrumental in moving you to action, from my experience the closeness of business associates or family ties seems to serve only as a mild catalyst for this development.

In reality, the closer you are to another individual, the less likely it is that that individual will be able to exert influence upon you. Conversely, an encounter with a person removed from your immediate general environment is more likely to stimulate change. A total stranger who passes only briefly though your life can spark your decision to act; an entertainer, politician or any other external figure can be the stimulus needed. You may be impressed and startled into action by unfamiliar concepts.

Bringing in an outsider can make a greater impact in shaking loose old habit patterns and ways of thinking and, in general, such individuals are often greater catalysts than are close friends or relatives.

When you intentionally seek out a mentor, it may be best to consider your selection as you might when selecting a board of directors for your company. You should seek out and select someone who has already experienced success in your area of interest, someone who would offer his or her candid comments. This person should also be willing to give time and talent to help provide strength for your endeavor.

I have had many mentors in my life who were outside my immediate sphere of influence, some who were able to take a direct part in my success and others who may not even have known of their influence on me. One person in particular was Dr. Fred Vogt. I will always remember one of his great lessons to me was to be decisive. Whenever someone would ask something of Fred, he would respond, "Yes!" He had learned, in most cases, people are very good talkers, but not many follow through on their ideas, so he thought why not give them encouragement right from the start. Observing his ability to make decisions was a catalyst for me to bring decisiveness into my life. So I received my DIN degree from Fred. Do It Now! If it's wrong or if it's right, you'll find out, but not until you get into action.

Remember, when finding a mentor you will want to:

1. Locate excellence in your field of interest. Find people who excel and learn from them.
2. Be attentive to overlooked aspects that could make a meaningful connection, such as harboring an erroneous, unconscious judgment or attitude about someone.
3. Expand your social circle by being inclusive, not exclusive.
4. Remember that like attracts like and that our tendency is to draw to us people who reflect our own image.
5. Realize that you possess both talent and skill. Tap into your talent by observing what you admire in others.
6. Listen with a critical ear. Listen not only to the words, but to the feelings of others. Criticism can be an extraordinary asset.
7. Your decision to act on an idea may be related to your mentor selection. Your mentor may be a complete stranger.

As the noted author and philosopher, James Allen, once stated, "Men are often interested in improving their circumstances, but they are unwilling to improve themselves. They therefore remain bound." Finding a mentor will open new doors of opportunity. You can choose your own course of action for fulfillment and growth, and there are people who will be willing to help you.

&

6

THE MENTOR MENTALITY

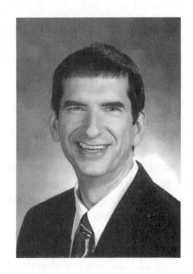

Jim Parker
314-503-3579
jparker@accessus.net

Jim Parker is a skilled presenter and consultant focusing on business development, communication and interpersonal growth. His passions have led him to create seven successful businesses within the last twenty-five years. Jim established The Mentor Connection in 1995 to help create empowering relationships through mentoring, seminars and consulting. His topics include "The Mentor Mentality," "The Power of the Breath"™ and "Mastering Interdependent Relationships." His clients include Ceridian Employer Services, Consolidated Communications, Illinois Power, Truck Center, Inc., and Watlow Electric.

Watching the Dream Team compete in the 1992 Olympic Games gave me cause to reflect back on all the times I watched Earvin "Magic" Johnson glide up and down the basketball court using what appeared to be natural, almost effortless, moves to baffle the other team. Johnson and I share the same hometown, Lansing, Michigan. I've followed his career from high school, Michigan State University and through his illustrious professional career with the Los Angeles Lakers. If ever a person was born with a knack for the game of basketball, it was Johnson.

Was Magic Johnson influenced by others in his pursuit of the game? That question was answered in *My Life*, a book written by Johnson with William Novak. Many people were key to Johnson's basketball success: his mom and dad; Greta Dart (his fifth grade teacher) and her husband, Jim (who was recruited to coach the fifth grade boys in basketball); Louis Brockhaus (his seventh grade coach); Paul Rosekrans (his eighth grade coach); Fred Stabley, Jr. (a sportswriter who gave Johnson the nickname, "Magic"); George Fox (his high school coach); Jud Heathcote (MSU head basketball coach) and Pat Riley (LA Lakers head coach). The list could go on. Johnson understood the importance of support, mentoring and coaching at an early age. He possessed what I call "The Mentor Mentality." He was inspired to win.

On November 7, 1991, Earvin Johnson announced to the world that he had HIV, the virus that causes AIDS. Johnson says in his book, "I was now playing a new position in a very different game. Instead of being a point guard, I was an activist, and especially an educator." As Johnson was being educated on HIV, he in turn was becoming mentor to the world on this critical issue.

The significance of "The Mentor Mentality" first occurred to me more than twenty years ago when I had the opportunity to compare results of two young men during their formative years, periods in their lives from the ages of twelve to eighteen. At twelve, these young boys had much in common, including similar upbringings, socioeconomic conditions and even similar outlooks on life. And like most twelve-year-old boys, they were very active in sports in addition to being excellent students. Each young man had a significant event happen when they were twelve. Boy 1 got into trouble by associating with the wrong kind of friends, became disrespectful to teachers and family members and his grades started slipping. He started skipping school.

Boy 2 also began associating with the wrong kind of friends and became argumentative and disrespectful. While at home one day, friends dared him to take off all his clothes and streak naked through the neighborhood. One of the neighbors saw him and called the police.

From that point forward, these two young boys chose different paths. Boy 1 continued on his path of self-destruction, becoming a ward of the court as he continued to miss school. In fact, he was thrown out twice and quit once. He left home many times during those years to live with relatives and friends and, at fifteen, he ran away to Florida. When the money ran out he returned home to continue his unruly ways. He was caught stealing cars and joy riding, and was arrested for being a minor in possession of beer. When it came time to graduate, Boy 1 finished 167th in a class of 167, with a grade point average of 1.5. He had to attend summer school in order to receive his diploma.

Boy 2, on the other hand, made different choices. He became interested in running and went out for track. As he trained he became capable of running a 4:30 mile. He joined the cross-country team and was ranked second in the city. Boy 2 had leading roles in three high school plays. He discovered a service club that he believed in and chartered it, a Junior Civitan Club, into his high school. He graduated with honors and a 3.8 grade point average. He finished high school in eighth place out of a class of 250.

What happened to these two very similar young men and why were their results so different? Boy 1 had taken a posture of "going it alone." He felt he didn't need anyone and he literally shut everyone out. Many of his actions were attempts to "get even" or to "show them." He made it virtually impossible for anyone to get close to him. When people tried he would reject them or hurt them in some way. He became an expert at shutting out the world. He was emotionally numb. When Boy 1 was asked what caused him to act this way, he said he "didn't feel like anyone really cared and they certainly did not ask for my input or listen to what I had to say."

Boy 2 attributes his change to "letting support in." His dad was accustomed to taking daily runs of three miles. Boy 2 got up one morning, not long after his run-in with the police, and asked his dad if he could join him. He became a runner that day and ran every chance he could get. He discovered that running with his dad gave him a chance to exchange ideas, get input, and be heard. This led him to join the track and cross country teams and he found additional support from his coaches and teachers. Boy 2 discovered a passion for conversation, for exchanging ideas, for voicing his views. When asked what the most important or significant difference was in turning him around Boy 2 felt "the biggest difference was active participation and support from my mom and my dad and my Junior High track coach." Boy 2 had adopted "The Mentor Mentality."

What is "The Mentor Mentality" and how did it make a difference between Boy 1 and Boy 2? "The Mentor Mentality" is a mindset, a way of viewing life, letting support in, a cooperative approach to learning, leading to true interdependence. The traditional definition of mentoring has been a unique, informal, one-on-one relationship between a wise elder who guided, encouraged and watched over the progress of a younger inexperienced person who demonstrated promise. In comparison, "The Mentor Mentality" utilizes a reciprocal approach. Those who embrace this approach have a passion for partnering with others.

The story of the two twelve-year-old boys is a powerful one for me because I experienced it first hand. This story is personal. I am Boy 1. And when my firstborn son, Boy 2, started down a similar path at the age of twelve, I realized that I had a chance to make a difference in his life and that I was committed to being there for him. "The Mentor Mentality" became a reality for me as I witnessed the changes in my son's behavior and in his results. He welcomed the support of others and became inspired to succeed. Reflecting back, it is difficult to say who benefited more from our mentoring relationship. My son, Jim (now a fourth grade teacher in Austin, Texas), and I still support each other whenever we can, professionally and personally.

Why is "The Mentor Mentality" so important? Mentoring has been around for centuries and yet it is more popular than ever. In my speaking and consulting business I have observed four reasons for this:

- Streamlined organizations
- Accelerated change
- Information overload
- Desire to give back

STREAMLINED ORGANIZATIONS

Every day we are hearing about companies cutting back or downsizing for a variety of reasons such as increased competition, deregulation, and market saturation. This is creating a need for each and every employee to be more competent, diverse, flexible and ready to wear multiple hats. Mentoring is providing a way for people to become competent at new tasks faster.

ACCELERATED CHANGE

All we have to do is look at the computer industry to get a feel for how fast things are changing. One of my mentors once said to me that change is happening so fast that often by the time a book is published the information contained in it is out of date. This is creating a need for more specialization. The fastest way for us to learn some of these specialized skills is to hire a "Techno Mentor," someone able to mentor us in the areas so critical to modern life, such as computers, communication systems, presentation equipment and even our remote controls for our TVs and VCRs.

INFORMATION OVERLOAD

It is easy to get overwhelmed by the increased amount of information being provided to us all the time. On a daily basis we are receiving information via mail, fax machines, e-mail, telephone, television, books, magazines and newspapers. One practical technique for integrating new information is to focus on what is important and have someone well versed in that area help us assimilate the information.

DESIRE TO GIVE BACK

The human spirit is naturally inclined to want to keep things in balance and to actively seek ways to share with others.

Regardless of the reason for the renewed popularity of the mentoring process, one thing is evident. It is building better working relationships through mutual support systems, teamwork, and cooperation on and off the job. One of the greatest resources we have today is the dedicated employee, with years of on-the-job experience, ready to help people who are just starting out. These employees are capable of working with their associates through formal and informal mentoring programs to accelerate individual progress and achieve results for the organization. Being around these relationships is one of the greatest perks of what I do as a consultant. It is hard to say who gets the most out of these relationships- the one being mentored (the mentee) or the mentor. I have found that many of our most experienced workers, at all levels of employment, are capable of mentoring and all we need to do is ask.

How can one adopt "The Mentor Mentality"? The following eight practices will lead to enhanced learning through successful mentoring:

- Become open to learning
- Establish a process of self-evaluation
- Recognize results
- Ask for what you want
- Make a commitment
- Be open to direct feedback
- Give back by sharing your own expertise
- Have fun

BECOME OPEN TO LEARNING

The first practice necessary in adopting the Mentor Mentality is to become open to learning. There is so much to learn: about life, love, work, history, politics, sports, the human body, hobbies, nature, the list could go on and on. The only requirement needed to begin is the thirst for knowledge. "Magic" Johnson was open to learning all he could about basketball. Learning doesn't stop with a formal education. It is a lifelong practice. With the challenges of our times it is critical to adopt a continual process of learning.

ESTABLISH A PROCESS OF SELF-EVALUATION

Before you seek the mentoring support of others, you must first be aware of whom you are. This process could be as simple as taking a notepad and going to a quiet space and asking yourself: What do I want? What do I need to learn? What do I do best? What am I passionate about? Answering these questions with honesty and clarity is a great first step in the self-assessment process. This should give you enough information to go forward or it may require that you utilize other resources to learn more about who you are. There are many resources available to help establish an

effective self-evaluation process including: visualization techniques, meditation, self-discovery workshops, breath work and
more.

RECOGNIZE AND RESPOND TO RESULTS

Recognizing and responding to results simply means altering
the course based on the results achieved. Evaluating results is one
of the best teaching methods available. Reflecting on results will
give you valuable information about your likes, dislikes, skills, and
abilities, as well as a true sense of what you are passionate about.
If you continue to do the same things, you will continue to get the
same results. It follows that if you don't like the results you are
achieving then you need to change your behavior. Recognizing,
evaluating and responding to results is a great way to stay on
course.

ASK FOR WHAT YOU WANT

This may sound simple yet it amazes me how many people
have trouble asking for what they want. Once you have opened
yourself up to learning and completed your self-evaluation process
you will have a pretty good sense of what it is you want to pursue.
Now the challenge becomes finding the people and resources you
will need to get the support necessary to accomplish your goals.
Then, once you find them, the challenge is to ask for what you
want. Fear of rejection keeps many people stuck in the status quo.
Having the self-confidence and certainty of purpose that comes
with knowing what you want will make asking for it much easier.
Once the mentoring resources have been identified and the support
has been secured, mentors will want assurance that mentees take
the next step.

MAKING A COMMITMENT

The single most important step anyone seeking a mentor has to
take is to make a commitment to the process. Whenever I am
involved in setting up formal mentoring programs with
organizations, this is the point I stress most. No matter how
anxious the mentor is to be there for you, the process will fail if
you do not make a firm commitment, first to yourself, then to your
mentor. This is why the previous steps are so important—you must
really know what it is you want and believe it will make a

difference in order to make the commitment to your success. If for some reason you are not able or willing to make this commitment, you have probably chosen the wrong path. Just go back to the beginning and look again at your self-evaluation. I cannot stress enough the importance of commitment! It is the difference between success and failure in any endeavor.

BE OPEN TO DIRECT FEEDBACK

The primary purpose of a mentor is to give feedback and support. This requires openness to what the mentor has to say. Practice the art of listening and taking in feedback. It is not always easy to take in this information. Yet if you don't listen to this feedback you will miss the golden opportunity to make the adjustments necessary to keep you on course toward achieving your goals. One practice, that makes this easier for me, is to ask for feedback. When I do this, I make sure that I am really ready to listen, as opposed to being unprepared to hear it. Listening to feedback will keep a person on track to meet goals and achieve results. This will also prepare you for the next step.

GIVE BACK

Once you maintain these aforementioned practices with regularity "The Mentor Mentality" begins to take root. Utilizing the first six practices successfully will set the direction necessary to accomplish objectives and create results. Now you are ready to give back. You are ready when you are open to helping others achieve what it is they want. Giving back perpetuates the mentoring process. Once you have a sense for what has worked for you and what has not, you will know the importance of understanding self and committing to this process. That understanding makes you an ideal candidate to work with others seeking a mentor. My experience with formal mentor programs has taught me that the best mentors are the ones who have been mentored successfully. Once you have been successfully mentored you develop a sense of openness and a willingness to share, as well as an ability to ask for support when you need it. This creates cooperation and interdependence, which are essential for success-ful mentoring.

HAVE FUN

Yes, that's right, have fun! Lighten up! Enjoy the process. We live in a world with much stress and pressure. "The Mentor Mentality" is a way to enjoy learning. We vastly increase our ability to build more meaningful relationships, make friends and network with people of like mind through mentoring. "The Mentor Mentality" can be applied in all aspects of your life, including recreation, providing a way to try many new and exciting things such as: flying, skiing, hang gliding, rollerblading, tennis, golf, travel, etc. "The Mentor Mentality" provides a fun and easy way to expand horizons. We never have to be embarrassed or shy about wanting to learn something new. "The Mentor Mentality" changed my life, and it can change yours. Perhaps the best part of this process for me has been the creation of the kind of relationship with my son that would encourage him to share this recent birthday sentiment:

> Celebrate! You were born today & we are the richer for it! Loving, wise, gentle, motivating, giving, funny, determined, brave & strong. When I was a kid I looked forward to your birthday because it meant a big party. Now I look forward to being with you and celebrating life, love & friendship & because of your teachings. You have truly been a mentor to me.
>
> I hope you have a great day! I love you so much & I am very happy I can share this day with a man who truly is alive!
>
> Peace, Love & Harmony!
>
> —Jim

7

MENTORS NEED WISDOM

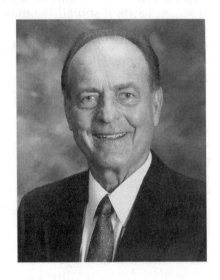

Michael Yessis, Ph.D.
760-480-0558
sptstrng@aol.com

Dr. Yessis has written eight books, more than 2,500 articles, and produced four videos. He writes regularly for *Muscle and Fitness,* as well as other magazines. He has been cited in *Sports Illustrated, Sport, Time* and *People* and has made guest appearances on the "Today Show," "PM Magazine," "Good Morning America," "Eye on San Diego" and CNN News. Dr. Yessis is president of Sports Training, Inc. a multifaceted company specializing in biomechanical/kinesiological analysis and sports/fitness specific training. He is also director of Strength and Conditioning at the Professional Golfers' Career College in Temecula, California, as well as Professor Emeritus at California State University, Fullerton.

According to the dictionary, wisdom means wise use of knowledge. It is not mere accumulation of knowledge but knowledge that has value or worth when it is put to practical use. The wiser the applications of your knowledge, the greater the success that you can achieve.

Few people disagree with this concept of wisdom, but all too often we do not see the full and worthy application of valuable knowledge. A partial reason for this is lack of sufficient knowledge. For example, what is ordinarily considered to be common sense really is an action or statement based on sufficiently sound information that allows you to come up with the common sense response appropriate to the situation. Wisdom can be exhibited only when there is a sufficient knowledge base. Knowledge by itself is worthless if it cannot be acted upon.

Coaches, who are often considered as great mentors, play important roles in the lives of many athletes. They usually have a good understanding of player psychology and the strategy and tactics that are involved in a game. But all too often they have little expertise in evaluating or developing the physical abilities of the players. They lack the knowledge and expertise in improving speed, quickness, power and agility of their charges.

For example, on a recent sports talk show, the former athlete and coach hosts brought out the need for the local professional football team to acquire players with good speed and lateral movements (as displayed by a Barry Sanders). I called to let them know that these qualities can be quite easily developed with professional level players. When I said that it is possible to improve speed and quickness, I was immediately cut off the air. In their minds, speed cannot be improved. Their "wisdom" was based on myth, not facts.

This is a classic example of how coaches may be experts in one area of the game, but neophytes when it comes to understanding other equally important areas. They exhibit vertical expertise, (i.e., deep expertise in one area) similar to a tall column. But, their breadth of understanding in related areas is usually severely lacking.

This is not true of the coach who has triangular expertise. At the base of the triangle is a wide range of information from many interrelated fields and sports. At the apex of the triangle is expertise in one area. In other words the coach is a generalist honed to a fine point. Because of his wide base of information, he is able to integrate many seemingly diverse bits of information to produce an outstanding product. He is not limited to one area as is the vertical expert.

There are many examples of vertical coaches who also serve as vertical mentors. Coach Ditka of the Atlanta Falcons illustrated this in his statement that if the players did not begin playing better he would quit. In his eyes, the players were already as good as they could be and improving the ability of the players was not his responsibility. Even the Florida Marlins baseball team mentors showed ignorance of player improvement when they paid close to 80 million dollars to buy the best talent available to win the championship.

This is indicative of the many owners and coaches who believe that it is necessary to buy talent since it is not possible to improve talent on the professional level. When you buy talent, the need for extensive knowledge or wisdom is not very important. At this time, only keeping the players happy and motivated so that they can play at their best is all that is important. It does not require a brilliant mentor to lead the team.

Vertical coaches even dominate the collegiate and to some extent the high school scene where recruiting is big business. Coaches believe that they must buy (the real name behind recruiting) good players in order to have a successful team. This is why some schools have multi-million dollar budgets for recruiting! The idea that they should improve the players from both a technical and physical standpoint, as well as teaching them the strategies that are involved based on their physical capacities, is for the most part, unheard of. Yet this should be the main role of the high school and, to a good extent, the college mentor if he or she is a true leader of young athletes.

When the coaches do not have the knowledge base to improve talent, many players fall by the wayside. When players do succeed, it is usually by trial and error and how much effort they put in, not through the knowledge and wisdom of their mentors. The coach can, however, be thought of as a good mentor in the eyes of the athletes, who usually do not have the knowledge to objectively evaluate them. But, the coaches can have great impact on directing the athletes to achieve success.

My first introduction to worthy use of knowledge or wisdom and the role of a true mentor came during my doctoral work in physical education with Professor E.C. Davis at the University of Southern California. He made me think of values and worth, not only of knowledge, but the true meaning of being successful. I read many books by world-renowned philosophers and leaders, especially those in ancient Greece. From them I learned that when sports and fitness activities become an integral part of your life, you appreciate and place a great value on them. The reason for this is that you derive the enjoyment and physical benefits that drive you on to seek more such adventures to get even greater enjoyment. The key is to become involved (show wisdom) and to learn to appreciate and experience the enjoyment and values of the activities.

With this outlook, I understood how the mere accumulation of knowledge, as so often happens in school as well as in our everyday activities, is not the answer to living a satisfying and successful life. Books that deal with health and other topics are usually based on the assumption that knowledge about fitness and health leads to the attainment of better fitness and health. However, learning about health or fitness does not lead to attainment of any substantial goals because knowledge alone is powerless as a motivator in human behavior. You must experience the knowledge; i.e., put it into use in your life!

From my mentor, Dr. Davis, I learned that most people want to be more successful in managing their lives, especially as they mature. This is where mentors or coaches play an important role.

My outlook on the role of knowledge changed from my work with Dr. Davis. When teaching physical education science classes on the university level, I strove to make sure that my students did not just accumulate knowledge, but that they understood and were able to apply the knowledge. Only in this way would it have some impact not only on their own lives, but on the lives of those with whom they lived, worked and played. Getting students to question the value of the knowledge acquired and to determine how it could be incorporated into their lifestyles was not only difficult, but very frustrating since most students were used to memorizing information and regurgitating it on the exams.

When students were forced to delve into why something was of value and how it could be applied and what it truly meant in the total scheme of things, it was for most students, a new experience.

Many thought it was a negative experience. My teaching evaluations were poor in comparison to the other professors, who taught in a conventional lecture mode. But it did not sway me from what I thought was the most important thing that I could convey to students to be truly successful in their careers and life. I knew that I was achieving success when I had many students come back after one or more years or after getting into the workplace, to tell me that what I had made them do in class was now making them successful in their chosen careers.

Further motivation in the area of gaining wisdom to produce a better person and athlete came from the Russians. Because my parents were Russian and I had a strong grasp of the language, my colleagues continuously asked me why the Russians were so successful in sports after they first appeared on the Olympic scene in 1952. At that time, I had no idea what the answers were, but through curiosity, I was able to get some literature from the Library of Congress which opened the doors to discovery.

I was so impressed with their work, I published a journal, *Soviet Sports Review*, which contained my translations of their articles so that coaches and educators in the U.S. could share in this knowledge. From my specialization in the scientific aspects of sports, I was well abreast of the information in this area, and knew the value of what I was translating. But the Soviet Union was our cold war enemy, and many thought the information was bogus.

However, the materials that I received were materials that were printed and published in the Soviet Union for use by the coaches and available to anyone who subscribed. Scientists share information regardless of politics! This was not propaganda material, although it too was available.

As I delved into the Russian literature, I was driven to learn more about how they developed their athletes since the information was much more advanced in comparison to other sources at my disposal. Instead of just being in awe of the material, I put the information into practice. I worked with various athletes and had phenomenal success in improving their performance.

If it was sound information, I made wise use of the knowledge that I gained from the Russians. Since I did not care where the information came from, and if it could be incorporated into the work that I was doing, it became useful information. However, it required sufficient knowledge to be able to incorporate this information into practical use to achieve success. Most coaches are not capable of comprehending scientific material because they do not have the training background necessary for assimilating the information. As a result, they are not capable of using the information to their advantage!

Mentor coaches often look for what they believe is the easy or the quick way to success. For example, I had a coach bring me his premier runner, who had world class potential, to analyze his training program. I made some changes and recommendations in regard to his exercises and technique that could have made him a world class runner. After approximately two hours of going through the material, the coach pulled me to the side and asked, "Since you know what the Russians are doing, what are the latest drugs that they are into?" He was only interested in pharmacology, not how he could use science to make him a better coach and his athlete a better performer.

The Russians, East Germans and others used drugs. But then who didn't? What was forgotten in all the talk about drugs, was that how one trained was extremely important, especially when using drugs. The drugs never did and never will be able to make an athlete great. It is the training that counts or, more aptly put, it is how well the information one receives and puts into practice (i.e., how much wisdom is used) that produces success.

Another aspect of working with athletes as a mentor is that the athlete (or student) be able to "stand on his own two feet". The athlete should be trained so that he can work as well as compete on his own. In other words, the coach or mentor should not have to hold the athlete's hand to help him make progress.

This was brought home to me in an embarrassing way on one of my trips to Russia. I was staying with a coach in Minsk when he said, "Mike, congratulate me, I just had my license renewed for another five years. One of my boys won his competition." I was somewhat taken aback, and asked when his athlete won. His response was "Yesterday. He won the pole vault meet in Moscow." I looked at him and said, "He was in Moscow, but you were here! Why weren't you with him?" He looked at me, wondering what in the world was wrong with me.

When he saw my surprised expression, he commented, "He doesn't need me; he's doing the competing, not me! I can't compete for him. Only he can do it, so why do I have to be there?" When I thought about this, it became clear. His task was to develop the athlete so he could compete on his own. The athlete does not have to rely on the coach as a crutch, but yet all too often we see this in the athletic and business world. The person is incapable of functioning on his own and needs someone to literally hold his hand in order to become successful. This can often be seen in the Olympic Games where athletes have their own personal coaches with them. It is as though without them, they would never be able to achieve success.

Through the wise use of knowledge, athletes and students not only gain knowledge of a particular subject, but they also gain an understanding of the knowledge and how it can be used in practical situations. With such understandings, they know what has to be done in order to improve. The athletes learn that they must do certain things on their own without the coach looking over their shoulder.

For example, when I would go out to the stadium in Russia, I would see the athletes come out on their own and begin their warm-ups and other activities well before the coaches took the field. When the coaches came out, they got together and the coach began practice. The coach did not take time to go through warm-up or stretching activities, since this was the responsibility of the athletes. If they did not do it, it would soon be apparent when the coach began working with them.

In talking to the athletes, it was obvious that they understood why it was necessary to do certain activities on their own. The rationale was explained to them, they understood it and with the knowledge that they had they were more than willing to do what was required of them in order to become better athletes.

By learning to work independently, as well as together with a coach, it is possible to learn not only responsibility but to develop the ability to improve without relying on someone to do something for you. In essence, the coach as a mentor becomes a guide, but you must do what is required on your own in order to succeed. Sadly, instead of looking to see how well potential talent can be developed, many coaches and bosses look only to recruit or buy proven talent to get the immediate benefits in regard to winning. This has its place but only for the present, not for the future.

Developing talent can be extremely satisfying. When I first coached tennis on the university level, I inherited some very good players who did not wish to work hard to improve their games. My philosophy has always been that in coaching the player should always strive to improve himself in order to be able to do the best job possible.

When my top three players refused to strive for higher heights, I cut them from the team and played the players who typically would not have played. We lost our remaining matches but in the following year, because of the understanding that some of the players achieved and with the work ethic that they had developed, one of them became the league champion in singles. This illustrates how it is possible to make great strides in one's improvement: This player moved from a #9 ranking to #1 on the team and in the league in one year.

Wisdom, putting knowledge into one's experiences or lifestyle, is an extremely effective way not only to bring about physical and mental improvement, but also to gain joy and satisfaction from the activities in which one participates. Understand that when you are able to accomplish a physical skill or accomplish a particular act, it is then that you receive the joy and satisfaction from the participation or involvement. If you cannot perform, then you will not receive the enjoyment.

Much has been said about how sports and other activities should be fun. I have often heard coaches telling their young charges to have fun. Fun, of course, is important, but I believe enjoyment and satisfaction are even more important. When you experience joy and satisfaction from doing the activity, you will come back for more. Merely having fun is a great pastime but it does not create a desire to work more or harder to continue playing or becoming better in a sport. I firmly believe this is why many youth and adult programs have failed. The coaches do not enable the individual players to achieve success, which is the key to building self-esteem, and to experience joy and satisfaction from the activity.

For example, if a youngster plays youth baseball, but cannot field the ball and strikes out almost every time he is up at bat, he will not enjoy the game, regardless of what else he gets from his mentor. If he hits a home run or has a base hit with men on base, he gets the joy and satisfaction of achieving this accomplishment. He does not have to be told he did a great job—he will already be experiencing the joy and satisfaction. Words of congratulations are icing on the cake! Thus, putting knowledge to use by having the youngster learn and master skills, which is not always fun, is the key to success in all endeavors. Very often the work that must be done to learn and perfect the skills is miserable, hard work!

Although I have written about wisdom in regard to coaching and improving physical performance, the applications are the same in other areas of life. The knowledge is different, but what a mentor and individual must do to succeed (i.e., exhibit wisdom) in business, family living, etc., is the same. When one learns the habits and the processes that one must go through, one can achieve success.

For example, when I first started teaching, I taught a beginning swimming class in which I required all the students to swim one mile without stopping and with no holding on to the sides of the pool. One of the girls in the class had extremely poor coordination and motor skills. Mastering the different strokes was extremely difficult, but, she persevered and practiced every afternoon after school.

At the end of the semester, she passed the test and came to see me a few days later. She said my class changed her entire outlook on life. She now knew that she could succeed at any task that she attempted. She had more confidence in tackling new subjects, had a more positive attitude on life and was transformed into a new person. She spoke of success not in sports, but in her other subjects and what she contemplated doing in her career and life.

Her story illustrates a most dramatic change but I have seen the same results from my sports work with people in Fortune 500 corporations and other successful businesses. I've noted that women, especially, who wish to succeed in their careers and in the business world, can develop the abilities to succeed quite dramatically. Through sports, they develop the skills, not only to be good in business, but also to participate equally with other businessmen, as for example on the golf course.

If it were not for my mentors, E.C. Davis and the Russian coaches with their advanced scientific methods, I would not have come close to achieving the success that I have. They made me see beyond the mere accumulation of knowledge and the mere relaying of this knowledge on to others. By closely examining the worth and value of the knowledge and how it fits into one's lifestyle makes the knowledge not only productive, but more enjoyable and meaningful. Knowledge by itself is a very poor motivator, but how it is used can be a very powerful motivator. At this time it is not mere knowledge but wisdom, and by acquiring wisdom, the limits are boundless. It is at this time that a mentor and his protégés are most successful!

&

8

BREAKING OUT

Ray Pelletier, CSP
800-SPEAKER
305-558-0500
raypellcsp@aol.com

Ray Pelletier is an international, world-class business speaker and the founder and president of the Pelletier Group, a management-consulting firm based in Miami Lakes, Florida. Author of the best-selling book *Permission To Win*, Ray is known not only for his "electrifying" platform presence...(*Successful Meetings* magazine calls him "a new breed of business speaker")...but also for his behind-the-scenes emphasis on solid, personal research into the specific strengths and weaknesses of client organizations. He has been called upon by such notable sports coaches as Lou Holtz, Dennis Erickson and Tom Osborne for assistance in motivating their teams to win.

Many years ago, there was a great magician and escape artist. His name was Erich Weiss. To give a demonstration of his artistry, he allowed himself to be put in a jail cell from which he said he would escape in twenty minutes. The constable closed the door of the cell and the twenty minutes started.

At the end of that time, he hadn't escaped. For the first time in his career, Erich Weiss—known to us as Houdini—had failed. But he was a pro and he stayed in that cell for *seven-and-a-half hours* before he finally called out, "I quit!"

The constable walked over, put his hand on the big iron door and just pulled it open. The cell door had never been locked. It was only locked in Houdini's mind!

Every athlete—Olympic or otherwise, as well as the rest of us—will understand exactly what that story is about. It's likely that at some point each of us has failed to achieve a particular goal because we approached it in the wrong way—we locked ourselves into a mindset that worked against us.

In my nearly twenty years of motivating corporations, coaches and sports teams to accomplish higher levels of performance, the mind-lock I've encountered most frequently has been my audience's preoccupation with the past. This obsession with "yesterday" can be pre-eminent self-sabotage. It promotes an attitude that often keeps them from winning in the present. I call it "December 31st thinking," and an excellent example of it is the story that follows:

Just before the opening of the 1997 college football season, North Carolina State (the Wolfpack) was universally considered hopeless. They were coming off back-to-back 3-8 seasons, they were plagued with player suspensions and bad press and they were twenty-five point underdogs in their season opener with thirteenth-ranked Syracuse. Nobody gave them a chance to put a winning season together, let alone win against the Orangemen—except Head Coach Mike O'Cain; he believed in his team, but the press, boosters, students and faculty didn't believe in him. In fact, it seemed very likely that his Head Coach's contract would not be extended beyond the coming season.

Two weeks before the game with Syracuse, O'Cain invited me in to help motivate his players. I'd never met the man, I knew nothing about him or his program and nothing about NC State. I familiarized myself with the Pack's record, did some research on the team and then went to Raleigh.

Very quickly, I came to realize that O'Cain might very well be the best football coach I'd ever known. I couldn't prove it by the Pack's record, and if I'd voiced my confidence in O'Cain at the time I'd have been laughed out of the State of North Carolina. He had quietly and methodically put a program in place that had every potential for making the Pack one of the best teams in the ACC. My years of association with winning coaches and teams enabled me to clearly see what many others couldn't—that O'Cain's thinking was real-world, his program was exceptionally well-grounded and his abilities as a leader and coach were outstanding.

Equally impressive was his character as a man, husband and father. He had everything it took to earn the respect and love of his players and turn them into winners. Despite losing seasons and wholesale lack of support, he'd quietly done what the very best of coaches always do: he continued to concentrate on the fundamentals...on the undramatic, long-term business of building a superior team. There was no question in my mind that everything was in place for the charge to a winning season and eventually to a bowl. The Pack was on the verge of breaking out—big time.

There was, however, one huge problem: his players didn't know they were winners. They had the right talent, the right coaches and the right program, but they had locked themselves into a 3-8 attitude; they didn't think they could win; they were fixated on their dismal record and past defeats. It was the only thing they could focus on.

My job was to get rid of that "December 31st attitude," not only in the players, but also in the minds of the coaches and Senior Leadership Council. They had to focus on a winning attitude with the same determination as the players and this called for more than a pep talk. Coaches and Council members had to buy into a new attitude, believe in it, support the players with it and stay with it throughout the season. In fact, after being welcomed to the campus by Coach O'Cain my first two formal meetings were with all the coaches and the Senior Leadership Council. I explained what I wanted to do and they picked up on it with enthusiasm. These were good people—they didn't like defeatism any more than I did; it had crept up on them and they just needed to understand how lethal it is and make a firm decision to flush it.

After that meeting, I met with the entire team. I immediately got to the point and told them I did not believe in 3-8. "You're better than that," I said. "3-8 happened yesterday. Forget yesterday. This is today. Your coaches know you can have a winning season. And from what I've seen of the program and your talent, I know you can have a winning season. Your coaches have decided you can go to a bowl. I've decided you can go to a bowl. But, you know what? It doesn't matter what your coaches decide. Or what I decide. The only thing that matters is what you decide. Not to decide is TO decide! You haven't decided to win. That's exactly the same thing as deciding to lose—and every team you'll face this season is down on its knees praying that's what you'll decide. But I know you're better than that!"

I looked around the room. "How many of you," I asked, "really, really believe you can go to a Bowl?" I didn't expect a positive answer and I didn't wait for one; I had no intention of debating the point. Right then and there, without any delay, I had to start building positive attitudes and enthusiasm, and it had to take hold and be contagious and spread throughout the whole team. I've found that the best way to do this with competitive athletes is to directly challenge them as a team; there's nothing subtle about it.

"From now on," I said, "every time you hear me say the word "bowl," I want you to shout it back at me: "BOWL!" And every time you hear somebody say '3-8,' I want you to dry-spit. 3 and 8 are bad numbers. When you hear them, SPIT! Those numbers don't have anything to do with who you are today. That's December 31st. This is January 1st. 3-8 is an insult! SPIT!"

In three seconds, the atmosphere in that room changed. "There aren't any losers in this room," I said. "You're just anchored to 3-8. You're tied to it. It's been drowning you."

I threw an anchor with a rope on it across the front of the room. They got the idea.

A couple of players had made the motion of spitting when I'd said "3-8." Some of the players had laughed. Then they'd all spat. It was taking hold.

I'd brought a couple of boxes of rubber bands to the meeting and I gave one rubber band to each player. I had two players take one of the bands and stretch it between them until it broke. "Easy, wasn't it?" I said.

Then I took back all of the bands from the players, joined the bands together and asked two of the biggest and strongest players to now try and break them. No way could they break those bands.

"We're like those rubber bands," I said. "As individuals, we can be beaten. As a team, working together, we can be invincible. A team is a 'we' thing...not a 'me' thing. And I mean on the field and off the field. You've given yourselves permission to win. Now give it to each other. Support each other, help your buddy solve his problems, work together, don't compete against him. He's part of you and you're part of him. I want each of you to take a rubber band and wear it from now on—night and day, until the season's over and we've won the bowl..."

"BOWL!" (Lots of high-fives.)

"No more 3-8 stuff." (Everybody in the room dry-spat. With gusto.)

A dozen times I used the word "bowl" in my talk that day, and a dozen times they screamed it back at me: "BOWL!" They were giving each other more high-fives—getting into it with enthusiasm. This wasn't the same bunch of guys who had come into the room an hour earlier. They were pumped! Not on your life would "3-8" ever again be anything else to them but an insult—that part of their lives was dead and buried. So much for the past.

And what were they thinking about now? It was the thing they had been screaming back at me—"BOWL!!" And what did that mean? It meant they had to have a winning season—something far better than 3-8.

Not a player or a coach left that room without the determination to make it happen. They walked out champions. It was what they'd always wanted to believe about themselves, but they'd needed a few phrases and visual props to turn that "wanting" into a beckoning reality. They WERE better than 3-8. They got it. They felt it. They could do this. They WOULD do it!

And they'd do it as a TEAM!

Yeah...they were ready! The underdogs had turned into the Wolfpack.

The confident enthusiasm stayed with them during the next two weeks of two-a-day practices. They practiced as winners, not losers, and they boarded the plane for Syracuse with real fire in their hearts. I was so impressed with their new attitude and their winning spirit, as well as with their coaching staff, that even though I'd been hired to do one program (thanks to Keith Harrell, a speaker friend who recommended me to Frank Granger, a loyal NC State booster and big fan of O'Cain's), I used my own dime to go to Syracuse and surprise the team by meeting them at the plane when it landed.

I was busting with pride over the Pack—the *new* Pack; they'd DECIDED to win! It was the only thought in their heads. I'd never seen anything like it! They were just as convinced as I was that they'd win—and I wanted to be there and support them and share their joy in an "impossible" victory over Syracuse. Like them, I had no doubt at all that they would achieve it.

I joined them on the bus from the airport to the Carrier Dome and put a Syracuse real estate guide on each of the seats. I told them I wanted them to get used to the town so they could see where their new house was—the Carrier Dome. I also wanted all of Syracuse to know that the Carrier Dome belonged to the Pack!

The police escorted the bus to the stadium with sirens blaring. (You should have seen the startled looks on the faces of the Syracuse fans at their tailgate parties in the parking grounds when the bus and police drove through! Some of them actually cheered for *us*, thinking we were the home team, until we drew alongside and they realized differently. It was great!)

I'd also had twenty signs painted with the word "WAR" on them in orange (We Are Ready). I instructed the Pack to remember that every time they noticed the orange "S" in Syracuse that was painted on the field they should think it stood for "State."

"And remember," I said to them, "you'll hear a lot of cheering in the stadium. Those cheers are for you. Believe it! It's YOUR house!"

When we got to the field, the ESPN2 crews were setting up their cameras and they started their broadcast by focusing on the rubber bands the Pack players were wearing—they zoomed right down on their wrists for all the world to see.

Then the teams took the field—and the rest is history.

Down 14-zip after the first quarter—no surprise to the Syracuse fans or the ESPN2 audience—the Pack came back to tie it and send the game into overtime. Syracuse made a touchdown and kicked the extra point. The Pack retaliated with a touchdown, and it was then that Head Coach Mike O'Cain made the decision he was born to make: he signaled the Pack to go for two points on the ground and win the game.

They went for it. And they won: 32-31! And anybody who saw it will never forget it.

Absolute pandemonium! An ESPN2 Director told me it was the first college overtime win, and perhaps the best football game they'd ever filmed. Later, ESPN2 used the game as a promo for their network—it was that exciting. "What a day!" said Pack Athletic Director, Les Robinson. "I don't think I can ever remember a bigger win for our football program. It has to be one of the greatest days ever for N.C. State!"

Coach O'Cain presented me with the game ball, but it should have been given to him for sticking to his coaching principles when he had almost no support and his job was very much in jeopardy. He was in hard place, that man, but he'd known the right thing to do and he'd done it. The Pack went on to a winning season (6-5) and O'Cain was given a new, four-year contract.

The Pack qualified for a bowl—but was not invited. That was a disappointment, but it was not a defeat; the championship program O'Cain has set up will not allow defeat. Defeat is refused admittance into the minds of Pack coaches, staff and players. They have one heartbeat, one focus, one vision—to build the program that will be a major force in the ACC in the near future. And I have every reason to believe they'll do just that. Not in my twenty years of consulting with head coaches and sports teams have I seen a team with a more indomitable will to win and a more total in-built refusal to cross the line from setback to defeat. Even their current season's 6-5 statistic is part of yesterday. It's part of December 31st and they don't think about it. They're better than 6-5. This is January 1st...and they're headed for a bowl!

"BOWL!"

I never come away from working with emerging champions without a profound respect for their common-sense acceptance of simple facts. All champions have that in common.

When it was pointed out to the Pack players, coaches and Senior Leadership Council, for example, that they were sabotaging themselves by locking their minds on yesterday's failures and that such a mindset was killing their chances of winning in the future, they quickly understood what they were doing to themselves. They acknowledged it without hesitation, they acted on it and they had a winning season.

Another plain fact is that we all want winning seasons and bowls in our life. It doesn't matter if it's in sports, business or personal affairs—we want to win. Of course we do. And to achieve it, we need to erase our own 3-8s in life and think "BOWL!" Do we see each new day as a fresh beginning—as a new chance to be confident and positive and determined to win? Or do we see each new day as just an extension of yesterday's failures and disappointments and low self-esteem? When we get up in the morning, are we getting up to December 31st or January 1st?

I constantly remind myself of this by taking a piece of soap and writing JANUARY 1ST on my bathroom mirror—it's right there waiting for me when I get up in the morning to shower and shave. By focusing on that undeniable fact and being determined to act on it, I arm myself with a positive attitude and an unconquerable spirit that is the greatest weapon for winning ever devised!

The bottom line for all of us is the same as it was for the Pack: winning *is* a decision—*not to decide IS to decide!* All of us need a game plan, just as a coach does, and a winning attitude—the firm decision to win—is the master key to making your game plan a winning one.

Lou Holtz, former Head Coach of the Notre Dame football team, breaks down the word "WIN" as follows: *W*hat's *I*mportant *N*ow. He's right. And he's talking to all of us. Hard work and a never-say-quit spirit provide a solid foundation for winning, but the most important thing to do NOW—whatever your game plan and wherever you are in life—is to BREAK OUT and DECIDE to win!

When winning is in your head, winning is in your hand!

℘

9

AWAKENING THE POSSIBILITIES

Rebecca L. Morgan, CSP
800-247-9662
408-998-7977
RLMorgan@aol.com
www.RebeccaMorgan.com

Rebecca Morgan is Managing Partner in Morgan Seminar Group, and an engaging speaker, seminarist and author from San Jose, CA. She works with organizations that want their people to work smarter and with individuals who want to get more done. Her seminar topics are Sales, Time Management, Communication, and Customer Service. Rebecca has authored four popular books, *Professional Selling, Life's Lessons, TurboTime, and Calming Upset Customers.* Additionally, she has produced numerous audiocassette programs and has been featured in Nightingale-Conant's "Sound Selling." Recently, Rebecca was featured in *USA Today, Home Office Computing,*

Sales and Marketing Management, and on National Public Radio and the Oprah Winfrey Show.

How noble to want to inspire others, but how presumptuous to think that we can do so purposefully! If we want to inspire others, we have to live our lives as someone who can elicit that response in others. We need to live congruent with our message. For example, if we want to help people live a healthy, fit life, we cannot eat donuts and fried foods every day and get drunk every night.

The meaning of the word "inspire" can be difficult to pinpoint. Here's the definition from the American Heritage Dictionary:

Inspire:

- To affect, guide, or arouse by divine influence
- To fill with enlivening or exalting emotion
- To stimulate to action
- To affect or touch
- To draw forth; elicit or arouse
- To be the cause or source of
- To breathe life into
- To stimulate energies, ideals, or reverence

What exalted definitions!

We know people who personify these definitions and regularly inspire others. How do they do this? What can we learn from them so we can be more inspiring to others?

LOOK AT WHAT INSPIRES YOU

To consciously inspire others, I believe it's important to examine what inspires you. Have you ever been inspired? What do you remember about the experience? What did it feel like? How was your life different as a result? Did you take some action, or did it change the way you thought? Who or what was the source of the inspiration: a teacher, a child, a clergy person, a leader? Or was the source internal—an inner voice that helped you through a tough time or helped you go beyond your previous limits? What effect did it have on you?

For example, I'm inspired by a player named Jerry Rice on the San Francisco Forty-Niners' football team. Jerry is renowned and revered in the football world, holding nearly all the records for his position of wide receiver. Jerry is famous for his personal habits that keep him on top professionally. A rare habit he's developed is to work out six to eight hours a day in the off-season.

This tough regimen keeps Jerry in such top shape that he is able to consistently out-perform his opponents. He bounces back from injuries so quickly that he hadn't missed a regular season game in thirteen seasons, until a serious knee injury kept him out of most of the 1997 season. But even with a serious injury, he returned to the game much earlier than the doctors had predicted.

Jerry is not just inspiring because of his physical routine. He has the ability to inspire others, on the team and off, to go beyond what they had thought they could do. This was acknowledged by his teammates voting him the winner of the Len Eshmont Award, given to the player who best demonstrates inspirational and courageous play.

What effect has Jerry Rice had on me? After all, I'm not an athlete so what relevance could he have on my life? As a speaker and author, I find that the thought of Jerry always looking for ways to improve has kept me focused on continuing to look for different ways to effect my audiences and readers. Jerry has a coach to help him run faster and jump higher. I engage coaches to help me fine-tune my speeches, to help me go beyond self-limiting thoughts, and help me write more effectively.

So, what is it that has inspired you? What can you learn from that inspirational source?

I find that to inspire others you have to first be inspired. Look at Mother Theresa, Nelson Mandela, Abraham Lincoln, Martin Luther King. They were all inspired, passionate, "lit up," about their causes. They were focused, even when things did not go the way they expected.

Perhaps our focus isn't global. Perhaps it's to make sure the children in our town are safe or that the people in our work group feel appreciated or that we share our talent with others. What's important is that we are inspired.

When exploring this topic with friends, a theme appears when we're inspired and we're awakened to possibilities within us. Perhaps we'd doubted our ability to do something, but were inspired when another accomplished it. Or we hadn't even imagined something was possible until we saw someone else achieve it, and we were inspired to go forward.

EXAMINE WHAT STOPS YOU

After identifying what has been inspiring to you, look at what has stopped you from acting on that spark. What happens when you feel inspired, excited, passionate, about something, yet it seems like a struggle every step of the way? Do you get discouraged, disgruntled, and depressed because it seems like you're not making any progress? Do you sometimes know that you're getting in your own way by not taking action toward your heart song?

When I've had the privilege of coaching executives, I've seen these highly accomplished people stop themselves more often than other people stopping them. While coaching Ralph, a CEO, I got an image of a mental roadblock he was facing. It was as if Ralph saw a wall stopping him from acting on something he thought was the right thing to do. But this action was a bit outside his comfort zone. He shared his inner dialog: "I can't do that. What would the Board think? How might the employees react?" This was a formidable wall, very high, and very thick. When Ralph came upon it, he stopped. "I could never get over that wall. And I can't go around it, because it's much too long. There is nothing I can do."

As the coach, I saw the wall from the other side. I saw right through the wall because it was a hologram! It looked exactly like a wall to Ralph, but I knew it was just an illusion.

Now my job, like every coach's job, was to coax Ralph through the wall. He thought, "I don't see how I could do it. What if I don't make it, others will laugh at my stupidity." And on and on.

Yet I knew that all he had to do was stick a leg through and he'd be on the other side in a nanosecond.

Inspiring people means not letting their thoughts build walls that keep them stuck. Or if they have "seen" the wall, then help them to force themselves through. Sometimes it takes the eyes of another to see these walls and coach us through them.

BE COACHABLE

If you're going to be inspiring to others, you have to be coachable. If you aren't, how can you expect others to be coached? When you are coachable, you trust your coach. You're willing to put your leg through the wall, even when you don't see how you can do it.

I've engaged a number of coaches. At first I found the relationship difficult. They would tell me to do something that was what I didn't want to do. I'd argue that their idea wouldn't work. I wouldn't be able to do it. I'd fail. Then I'd beat myself up.

Finally, with my health and fitness coach, June Anderson, owner of Fitness for Success, I realized that my way hadn't worked before so why was I arguing with her way? After all, I hired her to help me accomplish what I hadn't been able to do on my own. Although I knew what to do, I wasn't consistently doing it to produce the results I wanted.

As adults we have mastered certain areas in our work and life, and there are areas we know we're not competent. It was difficult, yet helpful, to think of myself as a beginner in areas in which I don't have mastery.

June knew when to ignore my protests, gently yet firmly urging me to do something that was simple to suggest, yet hard for me to actually do. She saw my capabilities beyond what I saw.

I was rarely exercising more than once a week. My goal in the beginning was three times a week. I didn't see how I could do it. I hated exercise. I was busy traveling, I was busy fulfilling projects for clients. Now I exercise much more than before. She coached me to go beyond what I thought was possible.

I felt embarrassed that I needed a coach to help me do things I already knew to do. "After all," my ego reasoned, "I'm a professional who runs a successful company, has written four books, and is in demand around the country. Why should I need a coach to get me to drink eight glasses of water or exercise? How ridiculous. I should be able to do this on my own."

The parallel to my own work struck me. Sometimes I remind people to do what they already know to do, but aren't doing it. My audience members are often intelligent, accomplished individuals who aren't doing what they know to do. I realized that I help them make commitments to follow through, to act upon the ideas we discussed.

Now I embrace the chance to be coached. I know that even Jerry Rice has a catching coach. He doesn't say, "Hey, I'm at the top of my field, I don't need anyone else to tell me how to do what I do best." His attitude is "Help me leap higher to catch this one."

It's not easy, but I think coaching is essential to being your best. Be willing to be a beginner toward mastery.

BE A BEGINNER

Inspiring people know that they don't have mastery over every aspect of their life. They are drawn to learn and grow and become better. They're willing to be a beginner.

What do I mean by "being a beginner"? It means being willing to try something new, something that you may not be good at, at least at first. Let me give you an example.

I was helping behind the scenes at a powerful nine-day personal growth program I'd attended the previous year. I hadn't assisted at this program before, so I was feeling new to everything.

As a participant, I'd felt that all my needs were cared for, never noticing the activity that made the program run so smoothly. Now, I was one of the dozens making it happen.

As a result of assisting, I had almost as many insights as when I was a participant. When the situation is right, learning can happen, even if the lessons come from watching your own arrogance, stubbornness, and pain.

One of the assignments I was given was to write down the participants' names as they shared with the group about their breakthroughs.

At first it was an easy task as one or two would stand at a time, with some time in between as others prepared themselves to share. Then the pace quickened with four or five in quick succession.

The pace kept up, and I got behind. I missed some of the names. The man I reported to pointed this out, although I already knew it. What I had remembered as a jubilant time as a participant, turned into a nightmare for me as a volunteer.

The next day, after sharing my frustration with a few fellow volunteers, they helped me see that part of my frustration was from feeling incompetent. I was in a foreign situation, asked to do things precisely, and then messing up a seemingly simple task.

I realized that I don't often allow myself to be incompetent—a beginner, if that sounds better to you. Although I try new things, they're built upon actions in which I've been successful.

I vowed to be incompetent—a beginner—more often, to learn and experience things outside my base of competency. Then I won't be so rattled when I'm faced with experiences far from my comfort zone.

Are you willing to be a beginner? Are you willing not to do well at something that seems simple? Are you willing to learn from the experience, not just how to do the job better, but how to be gracious even when messing up something important? I know I have a long way to go to become a master in this area.

LEARN TO BE YOUR OWN COACH

As you study with master coaches and surround yourself with people who inspire you, you'll learn to ask yourself the questions that they would ask you. You'll begin to prod yourself and ask tough questions of yourself.

One of my first coaches was a psychologist named Bob Goodenough. After I studied with Bob for a few months, he began to teach me to be my own coach. When I posed a problem, and seemed to be stuck, he said "What do you think I would ask you now?" I'd think about it a moment, then I'd ask a question. He would either help guide me further, or simply say "Great question. Now how would you answer that?"

I learned how to ask myself questions to get me through times when I was stuck. You can be an excellent coach for yourself, when you learn to listen to the voice that has your best interest at heart.

It's not that voice that tells you "You can't do it." "You're too old/ young/ fat/ bald/ short/ tall/ skinny/ dumb..." You know that voice, the one that seems to be shouting in your ear all day long.

Learn to listen to the quiet, calm, loving voice that tells you "Go for it," "You can do it," "Trust yourself." This voice is very powerful when you learn to listen and follow it. It's the part of you that has your best interest in mind. But we can usually only hear it when we're quiet, meditating, gardening, exercising.

When you act on that peaceful, wise voice within, you'll live your life congruent with your highest calling. And that is inspirational!

Listen to those who coach you to soar.

Not every "coach" has your highest good in mind, even though they may think they do. Listen to those who resonate with what you know is best for you and others. The story of my high school friend, Dave Mulligan, is the most potent example of this that I know.

At our ten-year reunion I watched him enter the room. In high school I'd harbored a not-so-subtle crush on him. I even volunteered to keep score for the swim team so I could watch him compete in his Speedos.

Even ten years older, he looked like a Greek god—he was "Bay Watch" handsome, his blond curly hair setting off his striking blue eyes. He'd become a carpenter, so his athletic frame was filled out with strong muscles. I'm afraid I clung too long as he hugged me hello. He seemed to have everything going for him.

Five years later, all that changed. He took his first recreational parachute jump. The jump was going fine until he was 100 feet from the ground. The person guiding him from the ground gave him conflicted signals. Go right, no left. At about fifty feet, Dave saw he was going to come down either into a row of cars, a trailer or a barbed wire fence. There was open space beneath him. It was his only chance. He needed to land quickly.

As he'd been instructed hours earlier, to come down quickly he pulled his chute's strings hard. Too hard. His chute collapsed. He fell 40 feet straight down. It was like falling off a four-story building.

Several vertebrae were crushed around his spinal cord. He was paralyzed from the waist down.

In the hospital after surgery, his doctors told him he'd never walk again. Although he had no feeling in the lower part of his body, he was determined to walk out of the hospital. When he kept insisting he was going to walk, the doctors insisted he see a psychiatrist to help him through his denial.

He was joined in his determination by his physical therapist, Helga. Every day she coached him: "Dave, wiggle your toes." Every day he tried, yet he couldn't. After each daily treatment, focusing on her words, he continued to try to wiggle his toes, determined to walk again. Helga didn't give up on him either, even though she knew what the doctors had said.

"You can do it; keep trying" she insisted. Every day she encouraged and caringly hounded him with her words. He would struggle to wiggle his toes every waking hour. "This is now my full time job," he told himself, "toe wiggling. And I'm going to be the best toe wiggler there ever was."

After three weeks of trying for countless hours, his left big toe miraculously wiggled. Hallelujah! This meant there was a neural connection from his brain to his toe. Soon his other toes were wiggling. There was hope for him!

Bolstered by his success, he worked even harder now to get his legs working. Helga continued her coaxing. After only three months, he was amazingly able to walk with the aid of crutches. He went from being a paraplegic to ambulatory in an incredibly short amount of time. He now walks without crutches and not only is happily married, but is the father of a little girl.

Dave's determination, buoyed by Helga's persistence and words of encouragement, helped him change the outcome of his life. If he'd listened to his doctors and not been inspired continually by the simple power of Helga's words, he'd be in a wheelchair, and have a much different life.

When he shared this story, he told me:

> It seems very difficult to motivate our mind and especially our bodies to do things that are nearly impossible. The power of thought—for example, seeing someone running and wanting to do the same—was the most effective healing power for me, but also the hardest to stay focused on. However the simple, constant chant of "Wiggle your toes, David" worked wonders to help continue that thought process and keep me focused.

We all have opportunities like Helga's—to touch people's lives.

In my life's journey I'm learning to be continually vigilant in my awareness and sensitivity not only to the effect others' words have on me, but to the long-lasting effect my words have on others. Author David Reisman said, "Words not only affect us temporarily—they change us."

Let's use the power of our words thoughtfully and positively to help inspire others—as well as ourselves—to go beyond perceived limits. "Inspire" may have lofty meanings, but it's worth working to awaken the possibilities within others. Who knows, we may awaken our own possibilities along the way. The key is living a life that is congruent with our highest good.

℘

10

INSPIRING THROUGH VISION & IDEAS

**Tony Alessandra,
Ph.D., CSP,
CPAE**
800-222-4383
619-459-4515
DrTonyA@alessandra.com
www.alessandra.com

Dr. Alessandra has authored thirteen books, recorded more than fifty audio and video programs, and delivered more than 2,000 keynote speeches since 1976. A marketing strategist and applied behavioral scientist, Dr. Alessandra is a leading authority on bottom-line marketing tactics and on building business relationships for life. Recognized by *Meetings & Conventions* magazine as "one of America's most electrifying speakers," Tony combines an endearing charisma and a command of his craft into a unique style that consistently captivates his audiences.

A kindergarten teacher asked a student what she was drawing. "I'm drawing a picture of God," the child quickly answered.

"But, sweetheart," said the teacher, "no one knows what God looks like."

"They will in a minute!" the child replied, according to a story told by Sheila Murray Bethel in her book, *Making A Difference*.

People who inspire others to win possess a similar, almost childlike faith in their vision and their ability to create excitement and change. People will follow a leader whose vision inspires them and makes their lives more meaningful. In fact, having a strong, captivating vision will go a long way toward compensating for a lack of some inspirational attributes. Einstein, for example, or Eleanor Roosevelt or Bill Gates, are not people who immediately leap to mind as charismatic leaders. But their strong ideas or vision may have more than made up for other shortcomings. (Have you heard the computer-industry joke? "What do you call a nerd fifteen years from now?" The answer: "Boss.") Their vision actually transformed them into charismatic leaders. The strength of their ideas and the passion with which they held them gave them a different brand of personal magnetism. Warren Bennis, author of the best-selling book, *Leaders*, says that being able to articulate your vision in a way that's easily understood, desirable and energizing is the spark of leadership genius.

WHAT DO YOU REALLY CARE ABOUT?

What do you feel passionately about? What do you care deeply about? Whatever your objective, whether it's ending world hunger or ensuring better care for stray animals, you'll never influence others to change their ideas or take action if you don't feel strongly about it yourself. How do you get such passionate vision? Well, the process probably varies somewhat from person to person. But for starters, a common denominator is to recognize what I call the need gap—that's the gap between what is and what could be. This disparity is the breeding ground for vision. This ability to see deficiencies in existing situations and act on them is one of the skills for inspiring others to win.

Consider Bill W. and Dr. Bob. As the founders of Alcoholics Anonymous, they started out in the 1950s in a small Midwest steel town with nothing but their own battered lives—and an idea. The simplicity of their twelve-step program, with its credo of "love and service," was a vision that has changed millions of lives.

Or take Carl Stotz, an almost penniless Williamsport, Pennsylvania, baseball fan who during the Depression liked to play ball with his two young nephews. Stotz wondered why the boys had to use clumsy grownup gloves, swing a bat that was far too big for them, and do an imaginary play-by-play "broadcast." So he acted on his vision. He found an unused lot and devised the dimensions of a kid-sized field. He asked around for other boys to play and other men to coach or maybe to umpire. He went to fifty-six companies before he found one willing to cough up the thirty dollars it took to field a youth team in 1938. He then persuaded local sportswriters to cover the early games and recruited friends, relatives, and fellow volunteers to build bleachers, embroider team names on uniforms, and perform dozens of other tasks. He drew up rules that would let all boys play, even if it meant having four outfielders rather than an extra kid sitting on the bench. His modest concept grew into-you've probably guessed it by now—Little League, a sports program that has affected more lives than any other. Baseball had risen from an old child's game in the nineteenth century to become the modem sport for the American masses. Stotz's vision returned it to the children. His vision, energy and hard work created recreation and character building opportunities for millions of young people and inspired many of them to win.

THE STEPS TO CREATING VISION

I think there are three stages to arriving at a vision that will help you inspire others to win. The first is your defining moment. That's when, as the saying goes, "the light bulb goes on." Something clicks in your skull. You realize you're on to something really exciting. This can occur in the throes of a busy day at work, but often it's a solitary experience. "If we are to survive, we must have ideas, vision, and courage," historian Arthur M. Schlesinger, Jr., wrote in *The Decline of Heroes*. "These things are rarely produced by committees. Everything that matters in our intellectual and moral life begins with an individual confronting his own mind and conscience in a room by himself."

Not every idea you have will be a breakthrough or a defining moment. Your idea might be initially exciting to you. But to qualify as visionary it must appeal to the values and the needs of the people you wish to inspire to win. So you'll have little luck in the long term if you merely have a solution in search of a problem, such as was represented by the infamous Edsel automobile, the "new" Coca-Cola or the rush to get the United States to adopt the metric system for all its measurements. These were all ideas that somebody had, but they were ideas that didn't fill a widespread need.

So, if you exaggerate the need gap or try to create a phony one, you'll lose credibility. What's required is some serious study to make sure you're filling an existing need, not a manufactured one or one that appeals to you alone.

Molly Wetzel's defining moment, for example, came after much work and worry. A business consultant and single mother in Berkeley, California, she watched helplessly as her once middle-class neighborhood fell into decay. A house nearby, owned by an absentee landlord, had become a haven for prostitutes, drug dealers and other criminals.

Her teenage daughter couldn't walk down the street without being solicited for sex and her young son was robbed of 75-cents at gunpoint. "It was a nightmare," Wetzel said. For eighteen months, she and her neighbors appealed to police and local politicians to no avail. Then one day she read an article about a California appellate court decision that declared small-claims court to be a proper place for settling disputes involving complex social issues. That was her defining moment. She knew the need, knew it very well. And now she knew the answer. Though she had no legal background, she soon corralled eighteen neighbors and together they sued the absentee property owner for destroying the neighborhood.

They won. Wetzel and the neighbors were awarded $2,000 each and within two weeks the property owner had evicted the drug dealers. Today the neighborhood is thriving—and so is the nonprofit organization Wetzel formed to help other neighborhoods fight crime by using small-claims courts or the threat of lawsuits, which is called Safe Streets Now!

"After we won the case, my phone never stopped ringing," Wetzel said. At last count, Safe Streets Now! had twenty-three chapters from California to Massachusetts and their actions had resulted in the shutting down of 485 trouble spots, including drug houses, liquor stores and motels that were hangouts for criminals.

Wetzel's efforts have been lauded by Harvard University's Kennedy School of Government, as well as others.

The real triumph, Wetzel says, is that neighbors learned the scope of their own power when it is based on action, both personally and collectively. New leaders emerge. "When they fight crime successfully, they realize that they can improve the parks and the schools—they can do anything." And the greatest lesson of all, she says, is that children watch their parents solve problems without violence. Molly Wetzel believed strongly in what she was offering, could explain how it filled a need and was willing to work hard to develop the idea and eventually she inspired others to win.

To truly influence others, you must have a mission. That's the second stage of fashioning a vision. It's what gives purpose, context and stamina to your defining moment. It isn't enough just to come up with a "mission statement" that merely sounds good or looks sharp on paper or in an annual report, though that's a start. Instead, to be effective your mission must come from your heart. It's got to grow out of a sense of what's important in your life and in your world. The deeper your passion for the mission, the more it will attract and inspire others.

Further, an effective mission must reflect the "need gap" by being sensitive to what other people want and need. The most effective missions involve helping others. "Leaders are more likely to be viewed as inspirational if they make self-sacrifices, take personal risks and incur high costs to achieve the vision they espouse," according to Gary Yukl, author of *Leadership in Organizations*. "Followers have more trust in a leader who advocates a strategy in a manner reflecting concerns for followers rather than self-interest." Thus, Bill W. and Dr. Bob weren't just helping themselves, they were inspiring alcoholics everywhere to redeem themselves. Molly Wetzel's mission was to make a lot of neighborhoods more livable, not just hers.

Choosing the mission often is what catapults people into a leadership role and puts them in a position to inspire others to win. Steve Jobs and Steve Wozniak didn't start up Apple Computer just to make money or to make people more efficient; their mission was to develop a "user-friendly" machine that would revolutionize people's lives. Their sense of purpose propelled them to perform brilliantly. And, characteristically, when they later sought to attract John Sculley, widely respected as a marvelous marketer, they didn't emphasize money or prestige, both of which he already had in abundance as Pepsi's president and CEO. Instead, according to Sculley's autobiography, Jobs and Sculley were walking near Sculley's home when Jobs asked, "So, what do you want to do, John? Do you want to sell sugared water for the rest of your life—or do you want a chance to change the world?" Sculley, faced with that kind of challenge and that kind of vision, knew what he had to do. He acquired a new mission and joined Apple.

CARING ENOUGH

Candy Lightner's defining moment came in 1980 when her daughter, Cari, was killed by a drunken driver. Her anger soon became her mission: the burning desire to do something about such wasteful tragedies. Within a few days, she held a meeting with a few friends—and that was the beginning of Mothers Against Drunk Driving, better known as MADD. Today, it's one of the most powerful citizen groups in the world. MADD has spawned hundreds of new laws against drunk driving in all fifty states, and offshoots, like SADD (Students Against Drunk Driving), have been formed to encourage further citizen action.

Candy Lightner had no position power when she began. Yet she is living proof of Andrew Jackson's famous epigram: "One man with courage makes a majority." Or, in this case, one woman. "If you care enough," Lightner says, "you can accomplish anything."

THE EVOLUTION OF A MISSION

You may have noticed a few things about the missions I've talked about so far. First, none of them—not Bill W. or Dr. Bob, Carl Stotz, Molly Wetzel, Candy Lightner or Steve Jobs and Steve Wozniak—were primarily motivated by the desire to make a lot of money or get their faces on, say, the cover of People magazine. Some of them may have coincidentally become rich and famous, but that wasn't their mission, and it shouldn't be yours. Second, probably none of them set out by telling themselves, "I'm going to be a leader with a mission. "Instead, their mission kind of evolved from what they were doing at work or at home or in their spare time. And then it grew and inspired others. If your mission coincides with your occupation, great! But if it doesn't, that may be okay, too. As Donald Clifton and Paula Nelson wrote in their book, *Soar with Your Strengths*, "If our work gives us purpose, then we have an advantage. But many people have a mission separate from their work, and their job is the means to support it." You may work as an engineer, for example, but spend your free time as an amateur pilot who flies doctors into Third World countries. Or having an aging, infirm parent may motivate you to get involved in seniors' programs. A woman I know gave birth to a severely disabled child and that experience led her to return to school, become a psychologist and specialize in helping other parents of handicapped children.

A POSITIVE ATTITUDE

When people or companies think only of how many units they can produce or sell, something happens to the spirit. "Painters must want to paint above all else," concludes noted University of Chicago psychologist Mihaly Csikszentmihalyi, who has studied peak performance.

"If the artist in front of the canvas begins to wonder how much he will sell it for or what the critics will think of it, he won't be able to pursue original avenues. Creative achievements depend on single-minded immersion. "Do you recall when Detroit automakers focused on how many cars they could sell rather than how well they could serve the American people with quality transportation? They lost enormous market share. As usual, your attitude can affect how you choose to frame your mission. Perhaps you look around and say, "Here I am, stuck in a dead-end job. How can I hope to improve my ability to inspire others to win? How can I possibly develop a mission?" But where we are or what happens to us is not as important as what we think about where we are or what happens to us. Maybe you work in a low-paying job at an art gallery. Looked at from a cynical perspective, you sell expensive paintings to rich people, and that doesn't strike you as either noble or a good base for inspiring others to win. But what if you thought of what you do as helping to spread beauty or as helping artists make a living and, thus, of spawning creativity? Or maybe you're an insurance agent, hardly a glamorous or altruistic role at first glance—unless you think of the families or businesses you're protecting, the financial safety net you're developing for all sorts of people. My point is, maybe we can't all have missions echoing the grand but simple nobility espoused by Salvation Army founder William Booth: "Others." But we can all look outside ourselves as we try to figure out our life's purpose. And looking outside yourself will not only help you to define your mission, but it will also help draw people to you and enhance your ability to inspire others to win.

FROM THE MOMENTOUS TO THE MUNDANE

Candy Lightner, Steve Jobs, and some of the others mentioned became, to some degree, national figures whose defining moments turned into missions and whose impact we can understand and perhaps applaud.

But vision doesn't need to spring from tragedy or aspire to greatness. It doesn't need to snare headlines or be cosmic in its scope. Your mission can mean that by just having faith you can accomplish something—and impart that faith to others. Take Edward Lowe. It's hard to imagine a vision more mundane than his. In the winter of 1947, he was working in his father's sawdust business in Cassopolis, Michigan, when he received a visit from a cat-loving neighbor. Her sand-filled kitty box had frozen, and she wanted to replace the contents with sawdust.

But young Lowe convinced her to try a bag of kiln-dried granulated clay he had in the trunk of his '43 Chevy coupe. It was a highly absorbent mineral that his father, who sold sawdust to factories to sop up oil and grease spills, had begun offering as a fireproof alternative. When the cat lady came back a few days later asking for more, Lowe knew he was on to something. It was his defining moment. He produced ten five-pound sacks, called the new product Kitty Litter, and offered them at 65-cents each. People laughed because sand, which had always been used for cat boxes, was selling for only a penny a pound.

Undeterred, Lowe gave away the ten sacks. When those ten customers returned, asking for Kitty Litter by name, it was Lowe's turn to laugh. A business, a brand, and a mission had just been born. Adapting clay for use as a cat box filler made felines more acceptable as household pets and made Lowe wealthy. Several years before his death in 1995, Lowe sold his Kitty Litter operations for more than $200 million. Meanwhile, cats had surpassed dogs as the most popular American pet, in no small part due to improved hygiene brought about by Lowe's innovation.

The third step, which is to have a breakthrough thought (a defining moment) and an overarching philosophy (a mission) will only get you so far. You've got to transform those thoughts and that philosophy into action. You do that by setting and accomplishing goals. You must not only believe you have a better sales plan, a better way to run the school board, a better solution for reducing health-care costs, an environmentally friendly mouse-trap, etc.

You've also got to figure out how you're going to accomplish your mission. So to bring your vision to reality, you need to present a strategy that is reasonable and attractive. That's the third step in creating and giving life to a vision. A goal differs from a mission. The latter is long term; usually, in fact, lifelong. But a goal is more time bound, existing only to be achieved. A politician, for example, might have experienced terrible poverty or discrimination as a youth (his defining moment). His mission became to enact laws that would right economic wrongs or free a whole class of people. But his goal would be, first, to get elected. Subsequent goals might be to get appointed to a crucial committee, introduce a strong piece of legislation, corral the needed votes, and so on. The mission stays the same, but the goals keep changing, as they must.

A PEAK PERFORMER PUSHES

The temptation is to set goals too low. Most people choose not to have high standards. But only by aspiring to be the best will you achieve high levels of success as well as the ability to inspire others to win. A salesperson may not want to make a call on a potential new customer for fear he'll be rejected. An athlete may not want to raise the bar for fear of failure. But the peak performer guards against this mindset. Nadia Comaneci, the first Olympic gymnast to score a perfect 10, said, "I always underestimated what I did by saying, 'I can do better.'"

To be an Olympic champion you have to be a little abnormal and work harder than everyone else. Being "normal" is not great because you may endure a boring life. I live by a code that I created that says, "Don't pray for an easy life, pray to be a strong person." Real champions know that failing with an excuse is simply not as good as succeeding.

"Only the best practice when they don't feel like it or when it is inconvenient," says Peter Vidmar, another Gold Medal-winning gymnast. "I made a clear list of objectives that I had to accomplish every day in the gym. If my workout lasted three hours, great! If the workout lasted six hours, tough luck! I wouldn't leave without accomplishing my objectives. My daily goal was to leave knowing that I had done everything I could."

Striving for and attaining goals makes life meaningful. Goals create drive and positively affect your charisma—but only if you set yourself to achieving them in the proper way. I've found that the letters in the word SMART are very useful in articulating goals. SMART reminds me that my goals must be Specific, Measurable, Attainable, Realistic, and Trackable. Specific and Measurable relate to how you phrase your goal. Vagueness goes hand in hand with lack of genuine commitment. You don't think a world-class pole-vaulter, for instance, just says "I want to jump higher next year." No, he has a certain height in mind. Instead of saying, "I will be more fit in six months so I can hike into the mountains and help with a reforestation project," you might say, "In six months my resting blood pressure will be ten points lower." Or "In six months I'll be twenty pounds lighter."

"I'll be running three miles in four to six months" is more effective than "I'll be running more in four to six months." Or if your goal is to become a standout salesperson so you eventually can rise in the firm and change its focus, you'd be better off proclaiming, "I will increase my sales next year by twenty percent" rather than "I will sell more next year." The terms "Attainable" and "Realistic" have to do with the goal, which should be just beyond your reach, making you stretch. It should be attainable, yet challenging. If it's almost impossible to achieve, a goal can result in loss of motivation.

On the other hand, a goal with a 100 percent chance of achievement is not really a goal; it's a given. And that defeats the purpose of goals, which is to move you forward by making you work harder or by gathering more resources than you have had in the past. And the "T" of SMART goal-setting is "Trackable." How will you know if you're making progress? You need to set up interim goals or checkpoints along the way. Depending on what your goal is, you might be checking your progress every day, once a week, or once every two months. You may discover that your goal is not attainable or realistic within the time frame you've set. But be flexible about your game plan before you reconsider your goal. Nothing ever goes exactly according to plan, so you may have to make adjustments in order to stay on track and keep up your motivation.

THERE'S HOPE

If you're not a gifted communicator such as, say, Winston Churchill, or you don't possess the panache of a John F. Kennedy or a Margaret Thatcher, you still can inspire others to win in ways big or small. In his excellent study titled "Leading Minds," Harvard educator Howard Gardner points out that our most famous leaders usually are "direct"—generalists who confront their public face to face. But others are "indirect" leaders who exert enormous impact through their ideas and the works they create. Creative artists, scientists and experts in various disciplines lead indirectly, through their work, while those who command institutions and nations lead directly in the more traditional way: public appearances, speeches, legislation and the like. In both cases, leaders relate "stories"—their ideas, their visions—which help establish their identities. Gardner contrasts, for example, Einstein, "a solitary thinker armed with only a succinct physics equation," with the powerful triumvirate of Stalin, Churchill and Roosevelt who met in Tehran in 1943 to plan a conclusion to World War II.

"Who ultimately had the greater influence?" he asks. The three strong world leaders changed, for a time, the world political map. But the lonely physicist, who preferred "the laboratory of his imagination," may have changed mankind forever. Charles Darwin led no organization, nor did Margaret Mead. Neither was a strong leader in the conventional sense. But their "visions," had, and continue to have, a huge effect on how we view the world and continue to inspire others to win, to this day. So, again, there's room for individuality in how you inspire others to win. Most of us won't found schools of thought, lead major organizations, or otherwise emblazon our way into the history books. But you and I can be the best people we can be and can inspire others to win. The surest way to do that is to first hone your vision.

A MISSION THAT MATTERS

Sheila Murray Bethel says there are three major roadblocks to creating what she calls "a mission that matters." First, thinking that you're too old or too young or too anything to have a mission; second, putting off getting started; and, third, doing nothing because you feel you can do so little. So there! That's the challenge: Get started on creating your vision, whatever it might be. As Helen Keller, sightless but inspirational to so many, once said, "I long to accomplish a great and noble task, but it is my chief duty to accomplish small tasks as if they were great and noble." That, in a nutshell, will help you inspire others to win—and win BIG.

℘

11

NOBODY DOES IT ON THEIR OWN

Shep Hyken, CSP
314-692-2200
ShepardH@aol.com
www.hyken.com/

Shep Hyken is a professional speaker and author who has been entertaining audiences with his unique presentation style for twenty-five years. In 1983 he made the transition from entertainer to speaker. He mixes information with entertainment (humor and magic) as he speaks on the topics most frequently requested by his audiences: Customer Loyalty, Customer Service, Internal Service and Customer Relations. His clients include American Airlines, Anheuser-Busch, AT&T, Fleming Food, General Motors, Holiday Inn, Kraft, Monsanto, Shell Oil and Standard Oil.

Inspiring others to win is the theme that runs throughout this book. Who has inspired us throughout our lives? Growing up, most of us had parents, teachers, friends, coaches and mentors who helped and inspired us. Just about everyone who has ever enjoyed success has had the influence and guidance of others.

As a professional speaker and author, I know what it is like to be on my own. I started my business when I was twenty-three. My first office was the dining room in my apartment. Eventually I upgraded to the room across from my bedroom. When I went to work in the morning, there weren't any cheerful people welcoming me as I walked in my office. Unless I picked up the phone to call someone, the only way to hear someone say "Good Morning" was to tune in to ABC's "Good Morning America."

My first speaking engagements came from picking up the phone and cold-calling potential clients. Youth and inexperience may have been part of what allowed me to overcome a fear of failure. Within a few weeks, I had started working with clients such as Anheuser-Busch, Enterprise Rent-A-Car and General Motors. My mother was so proud of me. She told all of her friends that I was doing it all on my own. She was wrong! (Sorry Mom!) I didn't do it on my own. In fact, I had *lots* of help. I had many mentors in my life. Some helped me by default, such as my parents and teachers. Others, I sought out.

I would like to share just a few of the experiences I have had with some of my most inspiring mentors. These experiences are probably not unlike the ones you may have had. Looking back and reflecting on these reminds me what I can do to help inspire others.

PARENTS

Parenting skills may be the most important mentoring skills we can have. I was lucky. My younger years were good ones. My parents could afford to expose me to many great experiences. They gave me a great home to live in, took me on family trips, sent me to camp, etc. Most important, they were somehow able to teach me to have appreciation for all of this while not taking it for granted.

In *The Nordstrom Way* by Robert Spector and Patrick McCarthy, a book about how Nordstrom's department stores do business, they talk about their hiring and training processes.

Nordstrom's is a legend when it comes to great customer service, and you would think they would have a very sophisticated training program for their employees. Yet, one of the best lines in the book is Blake Nordstrom's sharing of his philosophy about customer service training. He says, "There is nothing new in customer service. We are fond of saying that the best training you can have is (from) your parents. Did they teach you to be nice and smile and work hard? If you have those qualities, you'll succeed in our company."

As parents, we must realize that we are our children's first and most important mentors. Dr. J. Zink is one of my favorite authors on the subject of raising kids. The title of one of his book series says it all: *Champions in the Making*. Our children are the future champions of the world. We must take the time and make the effort to be the best mentors and role models we can be.

Let me pat myself on the back and tell you I was a pretty good kid. I wasn't a great student, but I also wasn't bad. I never did drugs or got into any real trouble. I attribute this to the way I was raised.

Looking back, here is what I remember. My parents taught me right and wrong—and more. They taught me why things were right and why things were wrong. And as I went into my teenage years, I was given a tremendous amount of independence. My mom says it is because I made good choices and she was able to trust me.

Ah, that is it! My parents knew the secret. They didn't have to tell me what to do. *They gave me what I needed to make the right choices.*

Teaching children to make the right choices is quite different from simply teaching children "right and wrong." They must be taught *why*. This reminds me of the proverb that goes something like this:

> Give a man a fish and you feed him for the day.
> Teach a man to fish and you feed him for a lifetime.

However, in this context that proverb might say:

> Tell a child, they know for the moment.
> Teach a child, they understand forever.

When my parents "taught me a lesson" (another way of saying "punished me") they gave me the "why" behind it. They didn't just say, "Bad boy. Go to your room." Realizing there is a consequence for bad behavior isn't enough, however. Even at a certain young age, we are able to understand a reason why certain behavior is bad. Once we understand, we can be taught to make the right choice.

FRIENDS

Again, I was lucky. I had some great friends. Toward the end of high school, I met a gentleman named Kim Tucci, a successful businessman and entrepreneur who owned a chain of Italian restaurants. I was seventeen and Kim was almost forty.

I had been an amateur magician, working birthday parties and nightclubs since the age of ten, and Kim hired me to work in one of his restaurants. I was successful and had set my sights on becoming a professional magician. This is also where I met Kim's partner, John Ferrara. Kim and John were great friends. Even though there was a big age difference, we really formed a great relationship.

When I was twenty years old, the president of our family business, Herb Wolkowitz, asked me to come and work for the family. At the time, there wasn't anyone else in the business. This was my grandfather's company and it was being run by Herb, who was an "outsider." This was one of the toughest decisions I ever had to make. You see, I thought I had already decided what I was going to do, and now someone was giving me an option I had never considered.

Kim and John spent the next day-and-a-half talking to me about the "decision." They actually took time away from their business to help me. The choice was to continue building my career as a magician or to give up everything I had been working on and practicing for the prior ten years to work in a business I knew nothing about.

The decision should have been easy. How often does the opportunity to go to work in a successful company with the virtual guarantee of becoming Chief Executive Officer come around?

But I liked doing card tricks at nightclubs! Obviously this is an oversimplification of the situation, but not far from the truth.

Kim and John gave me the pros and cons of both sides. They made calls to Herb to find out exactly what the plan would be if I went to work for him. After hours and hours of discussion, we came to the decision that I would work for the family business.

Fewer than three years later I found myself back with Kim and John making another career-changing decision. Without any input from me, Herb had decided to sell the family business. I remember being ushered into Herb's office to be informed of the surprising news. He said the market conditions were right and there was an incredible offer that couldn't be refused. At the same time I was told that I wouldn't have a job. Now I had to again figure out what I was going to do for the rest of my life.

Another choice was about to be made, but it wasn't as easy as the last one. Previously, there had been only two options, either continue my career as a magician or go into the family business. Now, I had no idea of what I should do. I felt as if the rug had been yanked out from under me.

John and Kim asked me a lot of questions over the next couple of months. What were the things I was good at? What did I understand how to do? We simply merged together everything I knew how to do well. By combining the performance background with knowledge of general business, we came to the decision that I should start my own business, doing what I am doing now—professional speaking and writing.

But I can't leave out the most important point. Kim and John never told me what to do, they just helped me gather the information I needed in order to make the choice.

BUSINESS

Starting a career as a professional speaker was fun. Some would say challenging is a better word to describe starting this type of business. But, I was very young—only twenty-three years old—which meant that I was inexperienced enough not to be concerned with rejection. I just moved forward, not even considering failure as an option.

First, let me tell you a little about the speaking business. You can start with virtually nothing. You don't need an office and an inventory of products to sell. You can work the business out of your bedroom, with just a phone and computer. You basically call up people and ask if they are interested in using you as a speaker at their next meeting. If they are, you send them information that explains what you do and, if you are fortunate, they hire you.

This is when another mentor stepped in, Bud Dietrich. Bud is now seventy-five-years-old, and we have a wonderful relationship that goes much further than his simply being a mentor to me and my business. I like to think of Bud as my "illegitimate" father. (Bud knows not to refer to me as his illegitimate son!) Bud didn't tell me what to do. He simply told me what he had done to make his business a success.

Bud knew about starting a business like mine. He started the same way. While the speech was the product, it wasn't the real business. The real business was getting the speech. Now this may seem obvious, but to most aspiring speakers it is not. Most speakers think that they have a great speech and people will simply call and book engagements. Unfortunately, unless you are a celebrity, this is not the way it happens.

Bud had discovered that the simple and obvious secret to success in the early stages of this business is to treat this like a regular forty-hour a week (at least) sales job. That was how he started.

I listened to him tell me how he became successful. He shared wonderful stories that I hoped eventually to experience myself. I didn't take his advice because he didn't give me any. He just shared his personal experiences with me. He gave me the information I needed to make a choice.

ON MENTORING

People seem to confuse the words mentoring and coaching. Mentoring is different from coaching. Coaching is about training, motivation, technique and "how to's." Mentoring takes coaching to a higher level. It is a relationship. Mentors may also teach and train, but they also set examples and model behavior. There is an old cliche: Those that can, do. Those that can't, teach. I'm not sure that I completely agree with that cliche, but it makes a point. Obviously, there are many great teachers and coaches who truly can "do," but they simply choose to teach. Yet, most mentors are sharing what they have done themselves. They tend to share what has been their proven track record of success. And the good ones know what other people have done to succeed and, unfortunately, sometimes fail.

You will notice a common thread in the three areas previously covered—parents, friends and business. It was all about learning how to make choices. But the learning didn't come from being told what to do. Yes, there was some of that from my parents, but the essence of it is that I was able to see my options and make my own choices. And the choices I made were based mostly on data.

Data is a strange word to use, but it is probably the best word to describe it. If we have others who simply share their relevant personal experiences, without telling us what we should and should not do, then we are free to make our own choices based on what we have learned about how others handled a similar situation.

Dispensing advice and saying things such as, "Like you should," "If I were you," "You ought to," etc. can cause resentment and defensive behavior. And what happens if the advice you give doesn't work? Then you have an excuse and someone to blame. But sharing experiences and letting people make their own decisions is a completely different approach.

A SPECIAL REQUEST

Throughout life we come into contact with many people who try to help us. Some spend more time with us than others. They are the people who inspire us to do more, make the right decisions and help us grow personally and professionally. They are our mentors. They are our family, friends and business associates. They are the people who have something to share with us based on their personal experiences.

Now comes a special request. There is no doubt that you have or have had a mentor yourself. Someone has helped you, inspired you and taken you under his or her wing at some point in your life. Now is the time to think about paying back. (Go along with me a little further on this concept.)

My friends Kim and John spent a lot of time with me. They didn't expect me to give them anything in return. I know because I asked them. But what they hoped I would do was give to someone else. When they were in their early twenties, they had someone who cared enough about them to share the wisdom and insight that helped them become successful. They simply wanted me to do the same for someone else—and I have. Now I am asking you to do the same thing.

Find someone who is at the beginning of something you do well, and help them.

Remember, mentoring isn't about giving advice. We can hire doctors, lawyers, accountants and consultants to give us advice. We can even write "Dear Abby." Mentors are people we admire because of what they have done. They inspire us because of their personal success. They can share that success with us, not by giving us advice, but by giving us information. They don't need to tell us what to do. They model their success. They can show us how they did it—by letting us in on the "how and why" of their choices, they can give us the information we need to make the right choices.

℘

12

CALLING ALL PARENTS!

Jim Brogan
619-584-0439
xclipper@aol.com

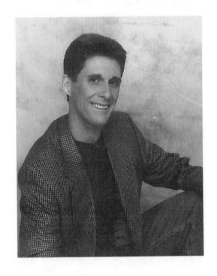

Jim Brogan has a varied background as NBA basketball player, professional speaker, instructor, author and financial analyst. He is a graduate of West Virginia Wesleyan College with degrees in business and psychology. He has delivered more than a thousand presentations to parents and children on the subject of life skills. He developed "The Making-A-Difference Motivational Youth Program," now in its second edition. Through audio tapes and a workbook, the program features a principle-centered approach to teaching nine- to sixteen-year-olds the skills of goal-setting and getting organized, and the importance of attitude, as well as other subjects related to success in life.

You and I are a bit alike, you know. We are among the three percent of American adults who read books like this because we have an interest in improving ourselves. We know that there are Olympians in our world in all areas: inspired goal-setters who succeed extraordinarily in their chosen fields. And we want to know how we can do it, too. We want a piece of that Olympian standard of excellence. Most of us believe that we have a chance at marked improvement or we wouldn't bother searching for answers. Luckily for us, if we are willing to supply the dream and the determination, there are many sources of self-help, including books, tapes, seminars, programs, groups, and even private consultations with experts.

The sobering truth, however, is that the same opportunities are not there for our most precious resource: our children. If you are a parent, you already know that there are programs available for *you*. Adults in general have many opportunities to learn effective goal-setting techniques in order to become smarter, more competitive, thinner, happier, healthier, better-liked, richer, more communicative—just about anything imaginable. Yet kids have startlingly few resources geared just for them.

After years of working with kids, talking with parents, and visiting schools, I have observed that parents and teachers who may be highly motivated talented individuals themselves, often throw up their hands in frustration when trying to motivate children to achieve. Kids can seem unreceptive and lost both at home and at school, and parents despair about "why Johnny doesn't care about achieving or giving his best."

A major part of the problem is the source of the motivation. Though it comes from the people who love them the most, advice from parents and teachers pales in importance when compared to the influence of peers and celebrities, especially for kids nine to eighteen-years-old. At this point, parenting seems to become a long-term challenge of olympic proportions!

What we need to remember is that for our kids, navigating successfully through the scary and confusing growing-up years in our fast-moving, complicated and hazardous society is at least as great a challenge. How can parents intervene to help assure a safe and positive journey for their kids? Parents must first find a way to ensure that their child is listening with interest; then they must ensure that the message sent and received is the right one.

GETTING THEM TO LISTEN WITH INTEREST

How then, can we reach kids, get them to listen, fire up their enthusiasm about setting and achieving positive goals, and spur them to action?

Let's look at two of the reasons that kids *don't* always listen to advice from home and school. As a result of working with young people for more than a decade, I have come to realize that part of the problem is *what* is being said and part of the problem is *who* is doing the talking.

THE "WHAT"

What is wrong with what is being said? Typically, kids are told to...

- Study harder
- Try harder
- Practice harder
- Make better choices
- Be more outgoing
- Get better grades
- Use your head

These messages are meaningless if youngsters are not taught and shown exactly *how* to do these things. In other words, kids often are not given enough information to set and achieve positive goals. They feel powerless to affect their own dreams or please their parents and teachers, so they stop listening to defeating adult messages and tune in to undemanding voices. Kids align themselves with a peer group that accepts them as they are. They idolize and emulate sports heroes and rock stars and actors who seem to "have it all together" because they have control over their worlds and the approval of millions.

This lack of effective communication between parents and children is destroying the strength of our families and the dreams of our youngsters. Research has shown the correlation between poor communication within the family structure and the social problems that threaten our kids: drugs, alcohol, crime, teen pregnancy, and school dropout rates. Yet, we can work on the quality of the content of our messages by making sure we are delivering effective examples and "how-to" strategies and not just sermonizing or admonishing.

THE "WHO"

That brings us to another reason our kids "tune out" the ideas of their parents. To young people, parents seem "to have all the answers" and to be very capable. Everything kids aren't. A tough act to compete with when you are an inexperienced, insecure kid who messes up regularly! And not a favorite source for more "lectures"!

Whether we like it or not, young people between 9 and 18 usually listen to advice from a "respected" third party with far more interest than they will listen to their parents, even though the parents are the ones who love them and consistently put their well-being first.

I know this to be true from personal observation and experience, but also from the tremendous response I get from kids who have used "Making A Difference," the motivational youth program I have developed over the last ten years.

The feedback I have received from parents also supports the strength of third-party advice. Whether it's because the kids know I played in the NBA or because they know I expect their best and tell them step-by-step how to get it, they do, in fact, listen and take positive action.

Perhaps it is because the program is *theirs*—it belongs solely to them. It is an arrangement between them and me, completely independent of school and home. The program arrives in the mail and is addressed only to them and is intended for their use only. Follow-up contact is directed to them personally. I have witnessed incredible growth in these kids, academically and athletically, socially and artistically, so I *know* they are listening! And after all, I am *not* their parent—a definite advantage. Consider using a third party as a motivational resource for your youngster.

SENDING THE RIGHT MESSAGE

Kids can achieve amazing improvement and reach wonderful personal goals if the right person gives them the right message. Most of us would agree that from CEOs to small business owners, from presidents to parents, we can all benefit from the interest and guidance of an effective mentor. As adults, we are capable of wise choices when selecting mentors.

When I was playing in the NBA, I knew I wanted to be the best professional basketball player I could be. So I asked Stu Lantz, a ten-year NBA veteran, to broaden my understanding of the physical and mental complexities of the game. I asked Phil Tyne, a strength coordinator for the San Diego Chargers, and Pete Babcock, General Manager for the Atlanta Hawks, to advise me on physical training so that I could increase my weight, strength and vertical jump. The results were not only exciting for me but also measurably successful! As an adult I knew whom to ask for help and how to approach them effectively.

But did you know that kids between nine and eighteen are afraid to ask for help? Your child will need your wisdom on this one. Be careful in your choice of a mentor for your child. The attitude of that coach, uncle, aunt, family friend, or professional can make or break your child's view of him or herself. Make sure that mentor shares your fundamental beliefs regarding your child's development and dreams. And remember, kids are as absorbent as sponges; they soak up outside influences forcefully. If you don't find a positive third party influence for your child, he or she will choose one for him/herself—usually a rock star, actor, or athlete whose beliefs and impact may or may not help your youngster.

GETTING THEM TO BUY IN

Okay, we now have your child listening, and we have taken pains to make sure the message will be the right one; but all of this effort will be for nothing if we can't get him or her to choose to act positively on the advice. Dr. Douglas R. Ramm, a clinical psychologist, after charting case studies for almost two decades, concluded that ninety-four percent of patients with self-inflicted wounds could be shown to be victims of their own ill-thought choices. We want our children to be the beneficiaries of the results of their life choices, not the victims. We want them to make wise and productive decisions in structuring their lives. We want them to buy in to the notion that *their* choices and actions have the power to make their lives better.

Most adults, and certainly most psychologists, would agree that there is a direct correlation between effort expended and reward enjoyed. We know that the more we work at something, the better the result will be and the greater the satisfaction we will enjoy in the end. However, kids don't feel powerful and capable and often don't understand that their own behavior and effort can influence the achievement of what they want and what they dream of becoming. Because they don't understand this, they fail to take responsibility for the actions necessary to achieve their goals. In fact, many of them are insecure enough to doubt their ability to take any action that will improve their lives at all!

In the "Making A Difference" program, I was careful to include a self-esteem building element that helps youngsters increase their self-confidence as they accumulate small successes from day to day. This makes kids receptive to the all-important "can-do" messages about positive attitude and helps them to benefit from the powerful influence of the high expectation held for them. *They must believe that they can do it (and do it well) before they can take responsibility for making improvements happen in their lives.* Parents can help by demonstrating their confidence in their kids' abilities through high expectations for successful goal achievement.

It has been my joy to watch youngsters I have worked with go through the steps to success: confidence building, positive attitude, high expectation, goal setting, hard work, achievement, and importantly, maintenance of goals.

One young man, in particular, comes to mind. He came to me during his junior year in high school. He was a tall, skinny kid and was tired of sitting on the bench during basketball games. I watched him sweat and work on his shooting and ball-handling skills when his friends were partying or sleeping late.

As we worked together month after month, I watched his strength, speed, skills and confidence steadily increase. I had told him that if he adhered to the program I designed for him, he would improve. Neither one of us imagined that he would lead his varsity squad in scoring throughout a victorious senior year, much less that he would set a new California State Record for three point shots made in a season! He went on to college on a basketball scholarship, and the record he set in high school still stands. All this from a skinny kid who came to believe in himself, was willing to work for what he wanted, and had the necessary guidance to make his plan work. This story repeated itself with the baseball player who dreamed of playing beyond high school and ended up at Vanderbilt University on a baseball scholarship. And again, with a young golf enthusiast who, with the proper guidance, transformed himself from a sixteen-handicapper to a college team player with a handicap of four.

Again and again I have seen the impact that motivational strategies can have on young people. *The most exciting factor for me is that these strategies are just as successful for kids with academic, social, or artistic goals for improvement as they are for athletics.* Of course, a critical element in all of this is the ability to set achievable goals that are meaningful to the individual youngster.

SETTING USEFUL GOALS/CREATING AN ACTION PLAN

Once your child "buys in" to the idea that his or her choices and actions can actually make a difference, it is time to set some personal goals. We cannot leave it to schools alone to teach our children how to set goals, maintain positive attitudes and behaviors, utilize motivational strategies, plan goal accomplishment and employ other elements of successful achievement. While many teachers make a real effort to at least touch on the subject, as schools take on more and more of the problems and duties of social work and counseling, it is unrealistic to expect that these areas will be adequately addressed. If you are a parent, you will need to be proactive in exposing your child to these concepts. Your child is going to need guidance from you or a third party in order to learn how to set and achieve goals.

I like to say that kids should dream big dreams once they choose their goals. The dream of Tara Lipinski was a big one, but obviously not too big to achieve—with good guidance and plenty of effort, as she proved by winning an Olympic Gold Medal. A goal has to be important to a kid before he or she will work hard enough to make it happen.

The goal should also be realistic and measurable, achievable in a reasonable length of time and within the child's physical capabilities. Often the guidance of a parent or mentor is needed to help a child define a goal in concrete terms. This is very important because *to truly set a goal it must be written down.* Then the objectives (behaviors) needed to achieve the goal can also be recorded. Time frames can be added. Space for logging results and noting adjustments should be included. What emerges is an actual step-by-step working blueprint for success that makes visualization of goal achievement more effective.

The action plan that results is exciting and motivating because it is specifically designed for their personal dreams, but also because it is designed to be implemented and managed by *them*. This last factor has the advantage of giving them control over their own lives, which is incredibly empowering to them and boosts self-esteem and self-confidence markedly while reinforcing a positive attitude.

A good example of the way an action plan works might be built around a child's desire to earn better grades in school. A period of perhaps three months might be set to measure progress. Objectives might include specific actions like:

1. Schedule fifteen-minute study increments broken by five minute breaks each homework night.
2. Arrange a time with teacher or tutor to get specific help before a test or on a certain concept assignment.
3. Ask the teacher for extra-credit assignments. All this should be committed to paper and a record of daily successes in achieving objectives should be a part of the plan. The child has major control over the implementation and success of the plan.

SKILLS AND VALUES

Now that your child is positively motivated and has a well-constructed action plan, he or she will need some basic tools. A significant factor in the successful implementation of a youngster's goal-achieving action plan will be mastering important skills for success, such as efficient organization, time management, and study skills. Different goals will require skills. As one example, in my program, all participants learn to use a calendar/planner system to their advantage.

The critical role of strong values' awareness cannot be overemphasized in your child's quest for success. No action plan will succeed without the presence of major quantities of responsibility, commitment, respect, accountability, determination and courage. A special dividend of the growth in personal character involved in nurturing values is a noticeable increase in self-confidence and self-discipline, which in turn make success all the more likely.

PREPARE FOR HARD CHOICES

Another important element in your child's success story will be a straightforward discussion of the negative choices that could defeat his or her dream. The use of drugs and alcohol can crush a dream with brutal finality. There is no doubt that illegal substances are available to kids today. And there will be other difficult choices relating to tobacco use, sexual activity, quality of friends, and activities to pursue. It is necessary that your youngster understand that he or she must be prepared and make a choice up front not to become involved with damaging ideas, people or substances. Peer pressure is an awesome force in influencing the behavior of kids between 9 and18.

Remember, the No. 1 fear for kids is that they will not be accepted as part of a group. It will take courage and determination, self-confidence and character to refuse to follow the crowd. But aren't those areas of newfound strength for a kid committed to achieving an important goal? In deciding to break away from the crowd on drug and alcohol issues, your child may find that he or she also has given someone else the strength to say "No." Your child's positive attitude may radiate such light that the attitudes of others benefit and change for the better. It has happened before, and it could happen again! It is an incredibly reinforcing experience.

I CAN! I SHALL! I WILL!

If I were asked the question, "What is the most important idea for young people to understand today?" without hesitation I would address my answer directly to the kids:

"Kids, every morning when you wake up you can choose to have a positive attitude that will paint your day in bright colors and offer you wonderful opportunities. When you combine your positive attitude of I CAN! I SHALL! I WILL! with an effective goal-setting plan and never quit, you will be unstoppable! And listen to this kids, if you put together days, weeks, months and years of choosing a positive attitude you will have found the key to a happy, successful life!"

So take heart, parents. There are ways to get kids to listen with interest, ways to motivate them to reach for their dreams, ways to reconnect with your precious child. Stay involved with your kids and make an effort to know their friends. Help to guide your children toward positive goal setting or find a third party to whom they will listen with interest. Your job as a parent is akin to an eighteen-year-long Olympic marathon! But as you know, the rewards far outweigh the pain, and my money is on your being equal to the challenge!

℘

13

YOUR MOST IMPORTANT SALE IS AT HOME

Warren Greshes
919-933-5900
Greshes@mindspring.com

Warren Greshes is a specialist in personal and professional development and President of Chapel Hill, North Carolina-based Speaking of Success. International audiences find that his practical "real world" solutions and views on the global economy are right on the money. His positive and pragmatic message has given thousands the power to overcome obstacles and conquer their worlds.

At the beginning of 1986 I made the decision that I was going to quit my job and start my own business as a professional speaker and sales trainer. This was a really big step, since I had spent my entire career working for other people. I had been a salesman, sales manager and then a division head for an apparel manufacturer in New York City's garment center. After ten years of that I had had enough, so I changed careers and went to work for a sales training and consulting company as head of sales and marketing. After a little more than two years of that, I decided it was time for the big step—my own business.

Upon arriving home one night, I said to my wife Linda, "I think I'm going to start my own business." Now, we had only been married a little more than two years and were planning on starting a family in the near future. In addition, we had just bought a larger apartment in our building in Manhattan and had taken on a pretty big mortgage. My timing was not perfect. Now, most spouses would have reacted in one of the following ways (and I would have been neither shocked nor disappointed if Linda had):

"Are you sure this is the right time for such a big step?"

"You have a good job, and you're doing well, are you certain you want to give all that up?"

"Maybe we should wait until we've saved more money and can better handle the mortgage."

"We talked about starting a family, maybe you should wait."

"Have you given this enough thought?"

Or, at least, most spouses would ask, "What kind of business do you want to start?"

Well, I'm proud to say Linda didn't say any of the above. All she did was turn to me and say, "It's about time."

Now that's what I call inspiration!

We are living in a time when people's lives are not only more hectic than ever, but changing rapidly. The last twenty years have given us:

- The proliferation of the dual paycheck, dual career household. (*Fortune* magazine found that eighty-four percent of two-parent households were also two-paycheck households).

- The service economy, affordable easy-to-use technology and corporate downsizing have created thousands of new entrepreneurs and businesses along with the end of the "I worked for one company my whole life" kind of worker."

Portable do it yourself pensions (the 401K) and soon-to-be portable health insurance now makes it easier for the American worker to change jobs.

What this all means is that it is more critical than ever for spouses, couples and life partners to:

- Have short and long term goals for their lives and careers
- Share those goals with each other
- Have total "backing and buy-in" of those goals from each other

There is nothing worse for a marriage, a life partnership or even a business partnership than to have two people going off in totally different directions. Or when one person doesn't stand 100 percent behind the other in a life-changing decision or venture.

I have seen more marriages and relationships ruined or severely strained because one person didn't fully believe in the other, or two people went in different directions totally wrapped up in their own lives and issues as if no one else existed. I actually know couples who have separate bank accounts for "His money," and "Her money." One of them might be saving up to buy a house, while the other wants to use what they refer to as, "My money," to invest in a business. To me, this is insanity. It's just basic common sense that two people working together toward a common goal will achieve a lot more than two people, who are supposed to be together, going off in opposite directions.

It's virtually impossible for a person to be successful in a new business venture or career without the inspiration and energy someone gets when they know they have total backing at home. I would never have started my business without it. Let's look at some of the instances that are quite common in today's society where inspiration at home is crucial:

- Starting a new business
- A career change
- Job transfer to another part of the country
- Deciding on whether to go back to work or quit a job to stay home and raise children

When starting a new business, chances are you're going to have a rough first few years. Every day that you go out in the world as a new business owner, be prepared to have your brains beaten out. Rejection will be your constant companion. The last place you need to have your brains beaten out or to be rejected is at home. Home has to be the place where you will get only positive reinforcement. It has to be your safe haven.

We had some very rough years when we first started our business. But whenever I would get down, Linda would invariably come up to me and say, "Just think about all the great stories you're going to be able to tell someday."

I spoke to a young man who had recently embarked on a new career as a life insurance agent. He told me he enjoyed the work, but his wife wasn't happy that he had to work a lot of nights. This is a typical example of what could be a rewarding career put in jeopardy before it gets started. Where are the shared goals? Where is the realization of shared short-term pain bringing long-term gain?

I told that young man that it wasn't his wife's fault that she was complaining about the long hours and the night work. It was his for not communicating to her what it would take on a short-term basis for him to be successful in the long-term. One suggestion I made to him was that he should take his wife out with him on some of his evening appointments. This would give her a better idea of what he actually did and how hard he was working. It would also show her that she had a role and a stake in his success.

In my first couple of years in business, I was away from home constantly. I would speak anywhere, whether they were willing to pay me or not, just to get exposure and, it was hoped, to generate some paying customers. Linda was home taking care of our newborn son and it was hard on both of us.

One day I decided to take her on a road trip with me so she could get an idea of exactly what I was doing. We drove from New York City to Hartford, CT, where we stayed overnight. The next day I conducted a full-day public seminar that I had promoted on my own. After speaking all day we packed up and headed to New Haven, where I delivered an after-dinner speech to a group of salespeople. We then got in the car and drove back to New York, arriving around midnight.

The next day Linda said to me, "You spoke all day and night. All I did was sit around and I'm exhausted. I can't imagine how you feel." This trip not only gave Linda an idea of what I actually do, but it also gave her a better understanding of the kind of sacrifice and dedication it was going to take, on both her part and mine. But most important, I think it helped her to see that she had as big a stake in the success or failure of our business as I did, even though she wasn't a full-time participant. Ironically, Linda now works with me full-time and owns fifty percent of the company.

If you expect total support at home I don't feel you can ever think in terms of "his" or "hers," or "mine" or "yours." It has to always be "ours." For one spouse to ask another, "When is 'your' business going to pay off so that we can live a better lifestyle," is demoralizing. There is no inspiration at all in that statement. In my opinion, once two people make a commitment to each other there can only be "our" because everything in their lives and careers overlaps.

Twenty to thirty years ago if a husband was offered a better job or a promotion that entailed relocating, it was easy. Sell the house, pack up the family and go. But it's a little more complicated now. The other spouse is probably working, too. That person might have an excellent job or own a business. At what point is one spouse holding back the other? This is where shared goals and an ability to think long-term comes in.

A close friend of mine was recently offered a big promotion. The money wasn't that much more but the responsibility was far greater and his exposure and reputation in the industry would receive a huge boost. The only problem: It was 200 miles away. His choices were to relocate the family or get an apartment where his new job was and commute between Albany, NY and Eastern Long Island. His wife, realizing what a great opportunity it was, was 100 percent supportive of anything he wanted to do. His children were not crazy about moving, especially his high school aged-daughter, which is understandable since this is a tough age for kids to be starting over, but they did fully support his taking the new job.

When they sat down and looked at their short- and long-term goals, they decided that as tiring and disruptive as a 200-mile commute can be, it was the best way to go. They realized this job was a stepping stone that would lead to even bigger and better things within two years and those bigger and better things would most likely entail another relocation. So what my friend chose was short-term pain (the added expense of an apartment during the week and being away from the family at least three to four days a week) for long-term gain.

Naturally, if he had felt he was going to spend the rest of his career in that job and location, the family would have moved. But he was only able to make these decisions and have these choices because he had 100 percent backing at home.

I think one of the biggest decisions couples and especially women are wrestling with these days is what to do after the baby is born—stay home or go back to work. It's the kind of decision in which full support and shared sacrifice is crucial. It's also the kind of decision that people often make for all the wrong reasons.

For instance, I've spoken to many women who would like to stay home with the children but decided not to because both the husband and wife felt they couldn't afford to lose that extra paycheck.

In many cases they're right, they can't afford to lose that paycheck, but in plenty of other cases they're wrong. They're just not willing to plan ahead or make the hard choices necessary. A good portion of that extra paycheck goes to the government. Another chunk goes to pay for child care; then there is clothing, transportation, lunches (at least $5 a day just for a sandwich and a drink) and let's not forget that $1.50 cup of "yuppie coffee" on the way to work. All of a sudden, living on one paycheck seems a lot more doable. Naturally, there is still some belt- tightening needed, but this is where the sacrifice and support come into play, in addition to the focused realization of what is truly important.

Many couples say they need that extra money coming in but then end up spending it on everything but the child (bigger house, European vacation, eating out, etc.). Then there are the husbands who don't want to lose their wives' paychecks because of the extra pressure it might put on them to earn more. If a mother or father wants to stay home and raise the children (stay-at-home dads are one of the fastest growing segments of the population), there is no reason it cannot be accomplished. Of course, there are many couples who don't want to give up careers or businesses and that's fine. The point is, if you really want a lifestyle change, prior planning, a willingness to sacrifice and a supportive spouse can make it a reality.

Recently I had the opportunity to be the keynote speaker for a large food products' corporation at their annual sales conference. I arrived the day before and attended their awards banquet that night. I sat next to a young woman who had just returned to work from maternity leave. The dilemma for her and her husband was that they both believed one of them should be home with their son, but she really enjoyed her job. What they decided was that he would stay home and take care of the baby. He restructured his job so that he could work part-time, work out of the house and if he had to go out and see customers, he would do it at night after his wife arrived home.

Linda and I faced this same situation when our son, Michael was born. Just before Linda got pregnant, we mutually decided, that she would quit her job and stay home with the baby. It was both a tough and an easy decision. Easy in that Linda really wanted to do it and I was all for it. Tough, because she was earning good money and I had just started my business less than a year before. How we managed was through smart planning and shared sacrifice.

We knew we had the better part of a year before Linda would give birth and give up her job. We worked like dogs in that time period, earning as much money as we could and saving as much as we could. We saved more than $20,000 in that one year and used it as cushion for the next year, because whatever I earned would have to support the three of us.

In addition, we sacrificed. No vacations—unless it was in conjunction with a speech and the client was paying. Eating out was cut to a minimum; the BMW was traded in for a Toyota Camry; the living room went unfurnished for a couple of years. We watched every penny. It was not easy but, of course, if it were easy, everyone would do it.

Our short-term pain eventually paid off in long-term gain. In four years the business started booming. Because of our sacrifice and our ability to live on one income, Linda was able to come into the business and work with me. This enabled us not to have to hire and pay someone from the outside and because we work out of the house, it still allowed Linda to be there with the children (our daughter, Emily, was born in 1991).

What made this all possible was a number of factors:

Shared goals—Both Linda and I felt strongly that one of us should stay home with the children. This enabled us to easily sacrifice material possessions to achieve that goal.

The ability to think long term—We both knew a few years of up-front sacrifice would reward us with many, many more years of long-term rewards and allow us to exert much more control over our lives.

Total spousal support—Linda sacrificed a lot of short-term material pleasures, not just to be a full-time mother, but in the hope that the business would grow. Never once, during the lean times did she question the business' existence, nor did she ever say I should get a job and give up. She had as much or more confidence in my ability as I had and she knew there was no way we would not be successful. That's true inspiration—the kind everyone needs.

℘

14

YOU CANNOT *NOT* COMMUNICATE

Francis X. Maguire

888-437-2656
HearthFXM@aol.com

Carmel Rivello Maguire, RRP

888-437-2636
HearthFXM@aol.com

Frank Maguire, as the original Senior Vice President of Industrial Relations of Federal Express is acknowledged as creator of the personnel, communications and employee relations programs that made that company the multi-billion dollar success story of the past two decades.

He served in the executive office of President of the United States during the John F. Kennedy and Lyndon Johnson administrations.

Maguire played a key role in the international expansion of American Airlines, and as Senior VP worked with Colonel Harland Sanders to launch the Kentucky Fried Chicken Empire.

He holds a Doctor of Business Administration, *Honoris Causa*, from Johnson and Wales University.

Frank Maguire is President of Hearth Communications Group in Westlake Village, California and Chief Advisor to Hearth Productions President, Carmel Riello Maguire.

BY FRANCIS X. MAGUIRE

It seems like just a few weeks ago when my young son Patrick and I walked out of the theater into the sunlight of a late Sunday afternoon. We had just spent a few hours seeing Robin Williams as a teacher in "Dead Poets' Society." I can't recall ever having been affected by a movie the way I was by that film.

"Did you ever have a teacher like that, Dad?" my eleven-year-old son, Patrick, asked. I stopped momentarily to think. "Why yes, son, I sure did. As a matter of fact, I had two teachers in high school I will never forget," I said.

The thought had been planted and the rest of the night I couldn't get Mr. Caruso or Mr. Flood out of my mind. As a matter of fact, they were still there in the morning when I got up. After the Monday morning paper and a cup of coffee I still couldn't get them out of my head. Maybe I should give them a call. So long ago...they would never remember Francis Maguire...why should they? Anyway, it was Monday and I had a million things to do. Important things like...forget it. Patrick had started my mind churning.

I went to the phone and called New York information for Xavier High School at 30 West Sixteenth Street. I couldn't believe I remembered the address after all that time. I asked for the alumni office and, sure enough, they came up with the two phone numbers of teachers who had been long-retired but, happily, were still on the planet. How do you call someone you haven't seen in forty years? You don't. It wouldn't be fair to them. As a matter of fact, it would only embarrass them and put them on the spot. I thought about it for a few moments and it became very clear that this wasn't about remembering forty years ago. It was about saying thanks for forty years of experiences and joy and pain—successes and failures. These two people had made a difference in my life and I wanted to say, "Thank you."

The phone rang three or four times and I was waiting for the answer machine to pick up. But instead, I heard "Hello" on the other end.

"May I speak to Mr. Joe Caruso?"

"This is Joe Caruso," said a voice I hadn't heard in four decades.

"Mr. Caruso, this is Francis Maguire from Xavier High School, class of '51. I thought about you yesterday when my son and I saw 'Dead Poets' Society.' As we were leaving the theater he asked me if I had ever had a teacher like that. Mr. Caruso, you probably don't remember me but I just wanted to call and say thanks. Everything I have ever done in my professional life has been influenced by those memorable words you used to say so passionately when you were returning those weekly quizzes."

"I have never forgotten them, and indeed you have spoken of them often to me as I grew into manhood and beyond. I still remember the fear and anxiety I felt as you fanned those blue books in your right hand and swept that arm across the entire room and thundered, 'I can't stand people who meddle in the mire of mediocrity!' Now that was powerful. I have recalled that weekly ritual thousands of times when I have found myself in a place where it would have been so easy to surrender to mediocrity. Those words often made the difference between my self-esteem and a feeling of failure. Oh, yes, Mr. Caruso, I did learn a little history, but more than that I learned the value of making a commitment to excellence. You were a very important part of my learning experience and I just wanted to say, 'Thank You.'"

There was silence for a moment and then I heard a tearful voice on the other end say, "Thank you so much, Francis. I can't tell you how much your call means to me. I do remember you and have often wondered what became of you. I am so happy to hear your voice. I would like to talk with you further but right now I'm all choked up. Will you call me again in a few days when I get over this rush of sentimentality?"

"Sure, Mr. Caruso. I will call you next week...And again thanks for all you did for Francis and Patrick Maguire."

When I hung up the phone I went into one of those trance experiences. I was sixteen again, full of enthusiasm and yet so fragile...confident and fearful at the same time. Forty years later Mr. Caruso was there and everything was going to be all right—I just knew it. To me he was an inspiration. Someone I could count on...who believed in me. A real mentor.

I repeated that same experience the very next day when I contacted Kevin Flood, my high school English teacher who "strongly" urged me to join the debating society. Me...an awkward, shy and unsure freshman in high school. I was so bad. I mean really bad, but he saw something in me that no one else did, and within four years I was competing in the American Legion forensic competition at Carnegie Hall. Now that was a miracle!

And there were many other mentors at various stages in my life. Men and women who took the time to look closely at what made me tick. Men like Harland Sanders of Kentucky Fried Chicken and Fred Smith, founder of Federal Express. Harry Keenan who treated me like his brother, as we planted the corporate culture seeds at FedEx...Hubert Humphrey, the man with the biggest heart I ever knew...my dear friend Don McCoy, the best manager I ever saw!

These and others like them had one thing in common. They were people who had faith in me. They validated me when others looked the other way. Life is all about validation. As Ken Blanchard reminds us in his classic book, *The One Minute Manager*, "People who feel good about themselves always produce good results."

And yet some people feel that the best policy is never to expect very much out of life. If you don't expect very much, their reasoning says, you will never be disappointed. It's people who think that way who like to lower the expectations of young people. If young people expect too much after all...the rest of their lives are likely to be one big letdown. If you ask me, that's a dreadful way to look at things. To me the danger of disappointment that comes from setting your sights too high, is far outweighed by the danger of underachieving that goes with setting your sights too low.

For most of us the major obstacle that stops us from realizing our full potential is our own underestimation of what our full potential is. We're too ready to accept other people's discouraging assessments of how far we might go and how high we might fly.

Seems to me the worst thing you can tell a person of any age is that he or she might as well give up pursuing a given goal because for one reason or another they'll never make it any way.

My "old" time friend, Charles Osgood, wrote a poem some years ago about a bird who never realized who he was:

A man once found an eagle's egg
And put it in the nest of a barnyard hen.

The eagle hatched and grew up with the rest
Of a brood of chicks and thought
he didn't look at all the same.
He scratched the earth for worms and bugs
and played a chicken's game.
The eagle clucked and cackled, he made a chicken's sound:
He thrashed his wings, but only flew a few feet off the ground.
That's high as chickens fly, the eagle had been told.
The years passed and one day when the eagle was quite old
He saw something magnificent flying very high
Making great majestic circles up there in the sky
He'd never seen the likes of it. "What's that?" he asked in awe, while
He watched in wonder and amazement at the grace
And beauty that he saw.
'Why, that's an eagle," someone said. He belongs up there, it's clear.
Just as we—since we are chickens—belong earthbound down here."
The old eagle just accepted that—most everybody does.
And he lived and died a chicken for that's what he thought he was.

The most important responsibility we will ever have as mentors is to stay in touch with the eagle within ourselves so we can help others whom we meet on life's path become aware of the eagle within themselves and realize their own "beauty within"—whether they are our sons, daughters, wives, husbands, students, friends or subordinates.

It's not that you *should be* a mentor—you *are* a mentor. To many people you pass on that road through life, you are a teacher. Think of the many people you have admired and respected in the past. They were your mentors. Some were conscious of that mentor relationship and the responsibilities that came with it. But whether or not you were aware of it, there were many others whom you watched from afar as they inspired you. You have heard it said many times and in many ways: "What you *do* speaks so loudly that I can't hear what you are saying."

We are all faced with a series of great opportunities brilliantly disguised as impossible situations. It's at times like these that the difference between success and failure may well be your mentor. Yes, it is true we all carry our treasures in fragile containers.

It's what we think of ourselves that sets our course in life and what we think of ourselves is often influenced by what others think. I was blessed with loving parents. Not every one is. But later on when I was out on my own, I met an old Jesuit priest who taught me a very important lesson. He told me that the most important act of faith we ever make is an act of faith to ourselves. I think God would agree with that. You must believe in who you are before you can be fulfilled as a human being. And yet how do you come to that realization? You learn from your mentors, parents, teachers, leaders, achievers, peers—people you admire and respect.

Are you aware of how significant you are to those around you? Not only your children or family but also your friends and associates, even passing strangers—individuals you might spend just one day with, one semester—one afternoon—one glance.

My partner, the co-founder of The Hearth Communications Group, was a man named John Culkin. He was so wise. He was always reminding us of our "strengths." He often urged us to turn off the "spotlight," which too often highlights the weaknesses and vulnerabilities we all possess, and turn on the "floodlight" so that we can see all the beauty that surrounds us and all the potential we possess. He put it this way:

> Everything you need to know,
> You know already.
> Everything you want to be,
> You already are.
> All the love and respect you crave
> Is available to you right now.
> And in that place,
> Where your fondest dreams take you,
> There are those who love you,
> Waiting for you to arrive.

Thanks John, you were so wise.

Each of us has so much to give. We communicate all the time. Too often we are just not aware of it. As a matter of fact, think about this for just a moment.

"WE CANNOT *NOT* COMMUNICATE"

We do it by our presence and by our absence,
By our silences as well as our words,
By our choices, gestures and attitudes.
We may not always do it well,
But we always do it.

How are you communicating? Are you aware of how important you are to so many people? You bring so much to the banquet table of life. Again, I remind you of so many great opportunities brilliantly disguised as impossible situations. And yet we survive and go on. At least most of us do. The question is, "Why some and not all?" The answer, I believe, is that some of us are inspired to go on by individuals whom we call our mentors—those men and women who keep us awake and aware of the fact that we are eagles, not chickens. Mentors—those who look for the light behind our eyes and who provide us with a wake-up call, because we all fall asleep at critical times in our life.

Dr. Benjamin E. Mays, the President of Morehouse College in Atlanta was mentor to thousands of students. His words were powerful:

"You are what you aspire to be and not what you are now. You are what you do with your mind, and you are what you do with your youth."

"Whatever you do, strive to do it so well that no one living and no one dead and no one yet to be born could do it any better." He continued, "It must be born in mind that the tragedy in life doesn't lie in not reaching your goal; the tragedy lies in having no goal to reach. It isn't a calamity to die with dreams unfulfilled, but it is a calamity not to dream. It is not a disaster to be unable to capture your ideal, but it is a disaster to have no ideal to capture. It is not a disgrace not to reach for the stars but it is a disgrace to have no stars to reach for. Not failure, but low aim is the sin."

As you journey through life, be aware of your significant place in the lives of others. As Robert Fulghum said in his book, *All I Really Needed to Know I Learned in Kindergarten*, "We need to hold hands and look both ways because we are crossing the street together."

One of the most brilliant minds of the 20th century was that of Buckminster Fuller. He would spend hours talking to his audiences about the fact that, "We are all on this spaceship earth together and there are no passengers; everybody is crew." How true that is.

The most important role each of us will play, whether consciously or subconsciously, will be the role we play as a leader—and leadership has more to do with character than it does with competency. As mentors, that's what we're talking about. We are helping our young students, sons, daughters and peers realize the importance of "character."

As I review my life, I think back at the opportunities I have had to help such talented people as Charlie Osgood at CBS and Ted Koppel at ABC launch their careers as electronic journalists. But I want to remind you of the people you never knew who were affected by you. These are the people who will be eternally grateful to you.

It's about inspiring others to win. It's about being a mentor. It's about being a communicator. No one wins without the inspiration of others and what a wonderful challenge we have to make this world a better place. That's a responsibility we all have and we should never forget it. You are an inspiration. It goes with the territory.

BON VOYAGE

BY CARMEL RIVELLO MAGUIRE

As broadcaster Paul Harvey would say "...and now, the rest of the story."

There was never a time I couldn't remember Francis X. Maguire and, every so often, throughout the past forty-four years, he would look out through the musty, crumbling pages of my high school scrapbook. Next to me at the camp picnic at Jones Beach, standing at my lifeguard station in front of the white picket fence at Whitestone Pool, smiling that shy, familiar grin of his.

So it was as if a small electrical charge went through me that day two years ago when I saw a picture of the keynote speaker for our annual convention at Balley's in Las Vegas. As Executive Vice President of Strategic Planning and Business Development for an international hospitality design firm, I was thumbing through the program book while planning my schedule for the three-day event.

I thought, "His name is exactly the same, but..." The years have a way of playing tricks on the way things were, appearance-wise.

I rushed home from my office that evening, pulled out the ladder and climbed up to the top of the stack of the boxes, looking for the special box I knew contained the memory-release I was looking for.

Two dusty, sneezy hours later, I was rewarded with pictures of "himself." The familiar boyish grin looked out at me once again, forty-two years later, changed somewhat from the corporate-looking, successful, charming gentleman whose photo I held in my right hand, trying hard to "computer enhance" the image through soft, memory-laden tears.

I called his room the minute I put my bags down in Balley's hotel. "No," he wasn't in yet, "but you may leave a voicemail message." An amorphous message straight out of James Bond followed. "If you are the Mr. Maguire who is the speaker for the resort convention, please ring room 2387 when you arrive...I want to welcome you on behalf of the American Resort Development Association" (didn't want any possible wife to get upset).

When I returned later that evening, the blinking light signaled "message waiting." The replay revealed a deep, resonant voice, stating that...yes, he was the keynote speaker, and...yes, please call room 1653 (will I ever forget that room number?) if you have a moment. *If I have a moment! I have a lifetime!*

When I placed the call later that evening, I heard a voice from the young girlhood I barely remembered—a deep, trained voice full of mellowness and resonance.

"This is Frank Maguire," he answered. With a rather dry throat, clutching the phone, I told him I was "looking forward to hearing his speech tomorrow..." which was titled "Corporate America's Wake-up Call"—great title!

"Could I ask you a few questions? Were you born in New York City?"

"Why, yes I was."

"And did you attend Fordham University, and were you the 'Voice of Fordham' on WFUV?" (no memory loss for this old gal), the answer was again, "Yes..."

"Do you remember Jackson Heights, Queens and St. Joseph's College for Women in Brooklyn, and Mary Louis Academy in Jamaica Estates?"

Words came tumbling out so fast that even I was surprised as the next question was blurted out.

"Do you remember a passionate Italian girl who was madly in love with you forty-two years ago?"

Silence for a brief moment, then....

"Carmel...is that you? Where have you been...I've been looking for you for twenty years!"

I will remember that exact moment for the rest of my life! I rode the elevator to the sixteenth floor and walked on unsteady legs clutching pictures of my four daughters in sweaty hands. When the big Irishman flung open the door, we hugged, cried and *I knew* that I had finally met my soul mate! We sat in his suite for three hours and spoke of our lives, children, past marriages...each of us having been single for many years.

We married on December 21, 1996, surrounded by our six children, family and friends—all of whom were as overjoyed as we were.

In the two years since we rediscovered each other, this man has been my most influential mentor. He has taught me how the world of business really works, adding his own expertise and spirituality, imparting knowledge gleaned from the years spent at Federal Express and Kentucky Fried Chicken and the White House, always with the patience of St. Francis, and always with a smile!

There could be no brighter classroom, no more comfortable chair, than in the school I now attend....I "learned all I really needed to know" in Maryland.

֍

15

NEGATIVE FORCES CAN INSPIRE

Jeffrey A. Isaac, J.D.
800-8Impact
619-588-2549
Jeffisaac@aol.com

Jeffrey A. Isaac, known as a relentless high achiever, focuses on a goal and does whatever it takes to achieve it. He has been an adjunct law professor as well as a successful trial lawyer for more than twenty-three years. He also has been engaged in numerous entrepreneurial businesses, before and during his legal career. A restaurateur, advertising agency president, and seminar leader, Jeff also is the author of eight self-help legal books, as well as various entrepreneurial books and tapes. In 1997, Jeff made the decision to retire from his law practice and devote full-time to developing seminars and products for new businesses.

Lying in the jungle surrounded by Viet Cong snipers—my world was suddenly different. At 19, I was experiencing emotions that most people never experience in a lifetime—feelings of panic, confusion and terror. Each time I moved any part of my body, I heard a crack from an AK-47 rifle, which hurled a bullet or two in my direction. I could only hope that it would not find any part of my body.

The year was 1968 and I was assigned to a communication center in Ban Me Tuit, Vietnam. We were in the middle of the Tet Offensive, a time in the war where utter chaos was breaking out all around us. I was ordered to destroy all of the secret communications in the communications center. The order came as a result of the immediate threat of being overrun by the Vietcong. Upon starting a bonfire in the middle of the compound, the Viet Cong snipers began shooting at me; all I could do was lay still behind a small barrier, and hope that the snipers would either be shot or somehow go away. The problem with their being shot was that they would tie themselves to the tress that they occupied, so even if hit or killed, our forces would not know it, since they would never fall from the trees.

That day I was provided with a significant inspiration on the value of life—mine to be more precise. I was barely out of high school and there I was, negotiating life and death. To compound the issue, my immediate supervisor, Sgt. Tucker, sat nearby viewing the incident, and instead of assisting in one way or other, thought the whole thing to be very funny! Well, one can imagine my chagrin. My life was before my eyes and my sergeant, whom I trusted and relied upon for help, was amused and couldn't care less about my predicament. To this day, I do not understand his reaction, yet, on reflection, feel that in war people act in the most weird and uncommon ways.

Yes, I survived the incident without harm; but came out of that situation with a very different and respectful view of life. I also realized that others were not always what they seemed, and were not always in alignment with the John Wayne movies that I grew up with.

Not only did I learn about life and about others around me, but it dawned on me that I received an inspiration that day—not in the traditional sense of having a mentor or of an individual leading by example, but, rather, through a reversal of the common form. I lived through an event that would change my life and I witnessed an individual's reaction to my circumstances that was totally inconsistent with my expectations.

These two events made me realize that my life was changing. You see, inspiration can be derived from an individual's action in a positive sense or one's reaction to an event or action in a negative sense. The internal reaction within you is the controlling factor, so that whether the event is a positive one or a negative one is unimportant.

The resulting reaction from a negative event can be just as powerful as that from a positive one—in either case catapulting you to levels never dreamed of. Your reaction to the people and events around you reveal everything about your character.

Upon discharge from the army, in surprisingly good physical and emotional health, I began college. I lacked some motivation and direction regarding where my life should go. After exploring various options and subjects, I made a decision to go into law and become a lawyer. I took the necessary Law School Aptitude Test and, due to my lack of talent for test-taking, I achieved a very low score.

Armed with my grades, character references and test results, and other relevant information, however, I made an appointment with the Dean at a prominent law school. After just a few minutes of discussion, the dean looked at me, frowned and stated in a dispassionate way, that with the test score on the LSAT test that I had achieved, I would never become a lawyer.

What an incredible statement! Completely negative and unconditional...but inspirational!!

Inspiration occurs within the receiver, not the giver, no matter what the intention. The internal reaction of the receiver controls the reaction and the value of the interaction.

Such a statement by a law school dean would probably send most people out that door into another venture. It had the exact opposite effect on me.

I had two choices:

I could have bowed to his expertise and advice and begun seeking another vocation. If I had allowed his remarks to dissuade me, I could have chosen to enter another field such as sales or computers. Had I been successful in that arena, subsequently I would have looked back at that day in the Dean's office and felt gratified that his words of wisdom righted my ship and provided a path away from potential failure and disappointment and toward another area more suited to my potential success.

Or I could have reacted the way I did.

Fortunately, I chose to ignore his advice. As I proceeded through law school, very few days went by that I didn't think of the Dean, his statement and his prediction of my failure. Whenever I was down or frustrated with school, that law school Dean was the major driving force that kept me going.

Bottom Line—I graduated from law school, tenth in my class, (ahead of most who had a significantly higher LSAT score than I had), received several awards, and continued on to a highly successful law career.

Inspiration comes in different forms. Inspiration can come from negativity—if it creates a particular reaction within yourself and provides you with the necessary drive, competitive edge or clarity, which otherwise might not have been catalyzed.

Whether it was Sgt. Tucker in the Army laughing at me, or the law school dean challenging me (without even realizing it) to seek a successful law career, the consequences are the same. People or events that move you, whether positively or negatively, are inspirational. Your internal reaction to an outside event, etched in your memory, is what will get you to a place that you might not have gone without such event or individual.

Since becoming an attorney, I have received much positive inspiration, which has helped guide my life.

As I have progressed through my legal career, I had always been drawn to attending seminars, listening to tape programs and reading as much as possible on self-help topics.

Every time I had an opportunity, I would listen to a self-help series and use the information either in applying it to my ongoing law practice and/or mentally file it away for my future ventures.

I have never been satisfied with the status quo in anything that I have done. Being a typical Type A personality, I knew early on that I would most likely venture forth to something other than the field of law.

In 1985, after gobbling up one self-help program after another, and attending numerous seminars and events, I pulled the trigger for the first time, and decided to venture into the legal self-help arena for myself.

Having purchased several self-help legal books published by No-Lo Press and having read books written by the master marketing and self-help guru, Ted Nicholas, I decided to sell my law practice and write "how-to" books on legal issues.

Armed with the information that I had received from my attendance of past seminars, I decided to write, publish, design and market legal books, providing the public-at-large with information and tools that would effectively eliminate the need for a lawyer. Topics such as "How to Do Your Own Will," "How to Write Your Own Contract," and "How to Put Together a Power of Attorney" were prepared.

Undertaking this project with very little prior experience was certainly a challenge, yet it was one that I was prepared to undertake.

By consistently focusing on the works and successes of Ted Nicholas and others like him, I knew it could be a successful enterprise.

Generally, the new business went very well, until I was persuaded to turn over the concept and, in fact, the whole project to one of the largest publishers in the world. I acquiesced to the idea that a very popular and highly respected publishing house would now publish me, and in so doing, the book's success would be assured.

How wrong I was! By giving up control of the business and relying solely on the publishing house, the business did a complete reversal, resulting in its failure.

Yes, I was inspired and followed the lead of my mentors, achieving success while I did so, however once I relinquished control the project failed.

I subsequently began anew, in a second legal career, and once again took up the practice of law for a period of ten years. Although I made good money in my legal practice, I never lost sight of my interest in self-help topics. Dr. Wayne Dyer was the next force in my life, which motivated me to go to the next level and follow my passion once again. I had followed Dyer throughout his career, and owned and read virtually every book and tape that he had authored.

In 1990, I had heard that Wayne Dyer would be appearing in Los Angeles, and I decided to attend. By that time, his influence on my life was significant. I respected the content of his books and tapes, as well as his background and persistence in achieving his goals.

I arrived at the seminar approximately three hours before the scheduled speech, and since other speakers were on the agenda before Wayne Dyer, I decided to have some lunch at the hotel nearby. As I entered the restaurant, I saw Dyer seated at a table eating lunch alone.

After debating the pros and cons of interrupting him and introducing myself as a "Big Fan," I decided to go for it.

After several enlightening minutes of discussion, Dyer invited me to talk to him again after his presentation. I did so, and actually became involved with his future presentations and developed a friendship with him thereafter.

This interaction was the precipice to the second ending of my law career and the commencement of my new career.

It's interesting that among lawyers, when gathered at their central meeting place, (the courthouse), the regular and routine discussion is how much they dislike what they're doing, and how they would like to extricate themselves from the law profession and go into something else.

Unfortunately, most just give lip service to this desire and never really take the necessary steps to fulfill their desire.

My desire to go on to something else, however, was strong enough for me to carry it out. My flame for movement into the arena of self-help and seminars was very hot and, in fact, had been fanned by the many who inspired me by their speeches and actions.

Hearing a motivational speech is generally not what really inspires most people, but the combination of the content of the speech with the actions of the speaker, is what true positive inspiration is all about.

The absolute joy of giving and receiving inspiration, when taken to heart, can significantly change a life—and that is probably the most rewarding feeling one can experience as one travels the roads and highways of the growth process. All of us certainly need inspiration at various points in our lives, to overcome the roadblocks that come our way, as we continue to strive for passion and excellence. As much as we need to receive inspiration from others, the gift of giving inspirational messages, whether orally or by action, completes the cycle, enabling our life to be complete and worthwhile.

℘

16

SHAMU & BEYOND:
THE PRINCIPLES OF
SUCCESSFUL MENTORING

Dennis Fox
800-989-SELL
703-904-7355
clientdev@earthlink.net

Dennis Fox is founder and president of the Client Development Institute, which offers training and assessments geared toward high-performance coaching and selling. A former top salesman for several national direct-selling organizations, he frequently speaks on the subject of hiring, coaching and performance improvement for corporations that include American Express, Airborne Express, Dean Witter, Hewlett-Packard, the National Restaurant Association and Sheraton Hotels.

The killer whales at Sea World know just what to do. A human hits the right keys on a waterproof keyboard, an underwater speaker emits a tone and Shamu or a friend jumps twenty feet into the air on command.

Those splashy feats are the culmination of a long, elaborate training process. I haven't mentored any killer whales lately, but the lore is that trainers start out with a bar at water level and coax Shamu into jumping above that height—where he *can't fail.* Shamu wins early and easily. The bar keeps rising, along with the whale's confidence, until it is at a tourist-awing level.

Over the past three decades I've trained thousands of employees for Fortune 500 companies, and I can't help thinking: "Imagine all the executives who wish they could press a few keys and get a well-conditioned rep to make a megasale." Can't positive reinforcement—the equivalent of a tasty fish or a tender pat on the snout—do wonders? Just break a job into child-easy steps and offer praise for good work and the rest will follow, right?

Still, as much as I believe in the Shamu Principle for mentors, it isn't a panacea. Mentoring us humans is far more complex than getting Shamu to jump above the bar. Even at the Shamu level we sometimes fail as mentors. We may stint on praise, for example, and confuse it with pampering. All too often we try to force a novice Shamu to leap over a bar ten feet high. That's why I'll mention this principle as my favorite, even if it isn't right for everyone.

But why isn't the Principle a panacea? Well, people can accumulate far more wisdom from experience than can Shamu and other creatures.

One of my favorite writers, Mark Twain, warned humans not to be "like the cat that sits down on a hot stove lid. She will never sit down on a hot stove lid again—and that is well; but also she will never sit down on a cold one anymore." With the right mentoring, those cold stoves won't be so scary. No, mentors can't control the environment and train students as if they were killer whales or kittens. But a good mentor can teach them to deal with failure and even thrive when the stove is hot.

So Just What Is A Mentor?

In Greek mythology the *mentor* was the guardian of the household in which Odysseus grew up. Today a mentor can be a personal coach or a manager in a role as a coach; I'll play up the second possibility here, just so you understand that mentoring employees isn't the same as managing them. No, you're working *with* them rather than bossing away. According to the *Random House Unabridged Dictionary*, a mentor is "a wise and trusted counselor or teacher" or "an influential senior sponsor or supporter." Would that more bosses paid attention. Notice the key adjectives, "wise and trusted." Clearly the word "mentor" suggests more than an ordinary teacher or an ordinary boss.

Here, then, beginning with the Shamu basics, are the principles of good mentoring:

1. "Praise, praise, praise" is to mentoring what "location, location, location" is to real estate.
2. Help people increase their "Aha's."
3. Lead by example—the sweat factor.
4. *Prepare* your people to be mentored.
5. Mentors beget mentors.

Principle #1: Praise, Praise, Praise!

I worked part of my way through Rutgers University by selling $400 sets of pots and pans during the scalding summers, in a territory that sprawled from southern New Jersey to the Pocono Mountains of Pennsylvania. My prospects were young girls who wanted to stock their hope chests. The decision to part with their $400 was not an easy one, and you might say this was a rep's equivalent of Paris Island boot camp.

Phil Monetti was a mentor of mine. He had a cleft palate *and*—not *but*—turned this seeming handicap into an advantage. What a masterful communicator and inspirer! As a mentor he was brilliant.

Back then I myself was obtuse. I helped oversee some other young sales reps, and I just did not understand why Phil heaped praise on them. The goal was to give two demos of cookware a night and hope for maybe three or four sales a week. Some kids could barely manage one demo a night, but Phil acted as if they were aces. "What?" he would exclaim. "You got a demo last night? That's great! Tell me how you did it." And if a hapless rep got no demo? Then Phil's jaw would still drop in seeming awe, and he'd say, "God, you worked the whole night even though you didn't get a demo! You should be proud." Phil just about would have congratulated the young trainees for breathing.

"Why," I asked, "are you rewarding incompetence?" And then Phil explained: He was buying time with praise. While the young reps were horrible by the standards of the pros, they were beating themselves—their best past performance.

Like most people, the young trainees were reacting more positively to praise and friendly pointers. Think of a waitress with a tray delicately balanced on her palm. Which is more effective—shrieking, "Don't drop that!" or saying: "You're doing great! Keep it up." Remember the old adage from sports:

Feedback is the breakfast of champions. When you praise, you earn the right to criticize. And be as public as you can be with your praise, and as private as you can with your criticism.

Also seek to be specific. Try to say *what* someone did well and determine *why*. Ask similar questions about missed opportunities.

Make your comments timely. A sales rep should have daily or at least weekly feedback—not just monthly feedback. Think of sports, of the thrill of seeing the scoreboard change lickety-split in a basketball game.

PRINCIPLE #2: INCREASE THE "AHA" FACTOR!

Sometimes the indirect approach is best, even with someone at the Shamu level—you can gently nudge people toward their own discoveries.

I think of the movie "The Karate Kid" in which a small boy asks a gardener to teach him karate so the bullies won't pick on him, and at the start the teacher asks him to do such chores as waxing cars. The gardener makes a semicircle with his hand to show how to apply the wax—and another motion to show how to wipe it off. The boy grows miffed. Shouldn't he spend more time learning karate and less time doing favors for the gardener? But finally the grand epiphany occurs. He realizes that the karate requires some of the same motions used to wax the car or paint a fence.

SHAMU & THE FOUR LEVELS OF EXPERIENCE

The young sales trainees working for Phil Monetti were at the first of four levels of experience.

Level #1: The trainee bungles the job and doesn't know why. This means you're better off just offering praise and, diplomatically, telling how Ellen and John can improve. They are at the Shamu level without full powers of self-discovery. Your trainees can't learn as much from their mistakes as they will later on. Because they don't know what's going on, you would be wise to adopt this attitude: "Anything that contributes to trust is worth the effort. Anything that doesn't—be careful!"

Level #2: Ellen and John themselves know why they messed up, and they're growing more confident and motivated. They can learn from failure. Ideally you'll encourage them to take yet more risks and remind them of the difference between knowledge and skill. Your trainees must not just learn. They have to do. In Silicon Valley, a past failure may actually help an entrepreneur get money for another venture—because he or she has learned and done. A venture capitalist once made a wonderful observation to a columnist for an online magazine published by Microsoft. "If I am given a choice between a guy who has failed a couple of times and a guy who is starting his first," said John Doerr, one of the Valley's leading money people, "I will fund the guy who has failed."

Level #3: The trainees succeed, but they don't know why. You need to focus even more on specifics and encourage your people to engage in more self-analysis. You should encourage trainees to come up with their own answers to ongoing challenges on the job.

Level #4: Ellen and John succeed and understand why they're successful. In fact, paradoxically, they have reached the point where they can succeed and not even think about it. More than ever, you trust them to be on their own. They're not just working for you. No, Ellen and John are working with you, and at times you even learn from them.

What a contrast this is to the tyrannical approach favored by some bosses—which often boils down to: "My way or the highway."

Sometimes self-discovery will mean that the employee works quite differently from the way that you do. But so what? As long as your trainee gets results without harming others, what difference does it make?

Be Socratic—ask questions to which the trainee can find answers. You may even want to use a technique of Carl Rogers, the father of client-centered therapy, and repeat statements as reflective questions. This can work out splendidly in the workplace.

Trainee: "I didn't do well last week."

You: (softly and without sounding sarcastic) "You didn't do well last week?"

As much as possible, get the trainee to ask the two most critical feedback questions:

- "What did I do that was most effective?"
- "Is there anything I could have done better?"

Each year our company, the Client Development Institute, trains thousands of people from leading corporations, and in our opinion, few questions are more powerful than those two. You need them to help guide the greenest novices in the right direction. And later the answers can help you see whether your wisdom has made an impression. Without self-analysis—continuing self-analysis—the trainees can never live up to their full potential.

Role-playing by mentors and students can encourage this analysis. When I hold training sessions for companies such as Merrill Lynch or Dean Witter, I play a broker. And some students play clients with me and with each other. That way, they can better understand the true meaning of client-speak. I ask, "Just what does 'I'll think it over' mean?" At first, some students may take it at face value. But then, when they're "clients," they realize that "I want to think it over" rarely means just that. Instead it's a polite "No"—or a request for more facts and maybe even encouragement. I let my classes discover this through an Aha! Experience. With the same goals in mind, I have students raise their hands to see how many take "I want to think it over" at face value. Fewer than a fifth of them do when they recall their experiences as real-life buyers.

And the hand-raisers learn from their classmates that they'd better change their ways—instead of presuming that real clients always think as they do. What a fine Aha! Role-playing is a wonderful way to introduce discussion of such issues.

Whether by role-playing or otherwise, you should gently get the trainees in the habit of analyzing their own actions. You can't shrink yourself, ride on their shoulders the whole day and whisper guidance into their ears. The trainees must find their own answers. Let them! When your trainees are ready, surrender control—so they can engage in their own truth-seeking.

TOWARD RIPKEN II: KNOW THY TRAINEE— AND CUSTOMIZE THE MENTORING

Who's the next Cal Ripken or Michael Jordan? Sports teams compile scouting reports to gauge the strengths and weaknesses of new talent. They try to puzzle out how prospects might fit in with the other players.

And the teams constantly track existing people, too.

Savvy corporations also hire pros to spot and evaluate talent. Paper-and-pencil assessments can help reveal a person's values and they can tell how he or she would express them in dealings with mentors, other colleagues and clients.

One assessment isn't enough. Best to evaluate not just values but also the expression of them.

In the values corner, here are the six most common values or attitudes, as described by the Personal Interests, Attitudes, and Values™ Assessment:

- *Theoretical. Classic quote:* "I will use my cognitive ability to understand, discover and systemize the truth." A Theoretical, as I see it, might thrive in Silicon Valley. She'd excel as a problem-solver. But without the right coaching, she might flop as a seller of high tech in Hollywood—where emotions so often prevail over logic.
- *Utilitarian:* "Every investment I make will have a greater return in time and resources." Meaning? You can motivate a Utilitarian much better with cold, hard cash than by giving him plaques and backslaps at company dinners.
- *Aesthetic:* "I will enjoy and experience the beauty around me and allow it to mold me into all I can be." An Aesthetic might do better selling in the upscale parts of town than in

ugly industrial districts. If he regularly beats his quota, you
might reward him with an office redecorated to please him.

- *Social:* "I will invest myself, my time and my resources in
  helping others to achieve their potential." A great candidate
  to be a mentor herself! A Social might even end up as a
  corporate leader if coaching fine-tuned her political instincts.
- *Individualistic:* "I will achieve the highest position and wield
  the greatest power." The true corporate politician—much
  more than the Social! The lure of rapid promotion can go a
  long way here. These people love to win.
- *Traditional:* "I will pursue and understand the highest
  meaning of life." Traditional types love to convert co-
  workers and clients to their spiritual beliefs. They can be
  strong allies and loyal workers if your beliefs coincide with
  theirs. See if you can't make The Product a part of their
  system. Of course, knowing why people do things is just one
  very important part of the puzzle. Knowing how these values
  show up in their behavior is another. The Managing for
  Success Style Analysis™ helps us gauge these patterns of
  expression.
  Examples:

- *The C. Analytical:* Tries to *control* the environment
  through analysis. Plays by the rules. Cautious. Accuracy-
  oriented. Jack Webb as Detective Joe Friday is the
  classic C—with the famous "Just the facts, ma'am." The
  circulation department at *Consumer Reports* loves the
  Jack Webbs of the world. So do corporate buyers of an
  analytical bent. Silicon Valley is full of Webb types.
- *The D. Dominant:* Fast-moving, interested in quick
  results. Beware of having a D work with a C unless they
  can adjust to their differences. Imagine the bad effect
  that an impatient, D-style rep could have on a Webb-
  type buyer who felt he was being pressured. But with the
  right mentoring, a D can fare much better with a C-style
  buyer than he would otherwise. The D can take extra
  care to do the homework—about products' specs, for
  example—that a C might demand.
- *The I. Influential:* Emotional and interactive—good
  talker but not the best listener. Joan ("Can We Talk?")
  Rivers is the classic I. An unprepared I may not fare well
  with a C who demands: "Just the facts."
- *The S. Security-oriented:* Seeks the status quo. An S is a
  hardworking, detail-oriented team player—the one most

> likely to wear a twenty-year pin and flaunt a family
> picture on his desk. So what happens when a dominant
> D on a deadline barges in and asks a steady S to speed
> up the project that he wanted to complete at his slower
> pace? Best to educate a D regarding the mindset of the S,
> and vice versa.

Yes, mentors can also gain insights by interviewing trainees or observing behavior on the job. But pencil-and-paper assessments, scored by computer, will offer a real edge here in developing talent. It's as if someone is using a tractor rather than a horse and mule to prepare a field for planting.

Needless to say, the right assessments can be of special help to the mentors themselves. They can provide a psychological benchmark, so to speak, and help you evaluate others more skillfully by knowing yourself better. It helps us to break the pattern of always asking, "Why aren't you more like me?"

PRINCIPLE #3: LEAD BY EXAMPLE— THE SWEAT FACTOR

This is pretty self-explanatory, but how often do mentors forget these basics? You don't have to be Lawrence Olivier to be a good acting coach. You merely need to know what rings true and how to challenge your students to achieve it. But it does help if—in showing your equivalent of a scene—you actually *act*. That way, you won't just communicate information. You'll also impart inspiration.

With the above in mind, I'm hardly surprised that Israel has one of the best armies in the world. When war breaks out, nervous young men in some countries strive to be military officers to avoid dodging bullets as often as the privates would. That strategy won't work in Israel, however. If you're an Israeli officer, you actually have more chance of dying on the battlefield than if you're in the rank and file. The battle cry of Israeli officers isn't "Forward, troops." It's *Acharai,* or *After me.*

I've used the same principle, the sweat factor, in my own work. Years ago when I was coaching automotive salespeople, I bungled around on the showroom floor. Barely able to distinguish a carburetor from a taillight, I didn't exactly rake in thousands in commissions. But unbeknownst to me at first, I won the respect of the sales team by risking failure. Several of the salespeople eventually confided, "I can't believe you hung in there so long." They themselves did not want to risk looking bad in front of their colleagues. As one of the troops, I couldn't lose. Bumbling along, oblivious to the real priorities, I had passed an unwritten test of courage.

PRINCIPLE #4: *PREPARE* YOUR PEOPLE TO BE MENTORED

Often people ask me, "Why doesn't training stick? How come intelligent people can so quickly forget what they're taught?" I answer with two questions:

- Which person can most determine the success of mentoring? The trainee? The trainer? The manager?
- What's the time that matters the most?

Did you think that the trainee is the person most responsible for the success of training? Me, too. I believe that *we* are the true masters of our fate. But research by Mary L. Broad and John W. Newstrom, the authors of an authoritative book titled, *The Transfer of Training,* indicates otherwise. The proper answer? The Manager. You, in other words. *You're* the one who'll encourage self-analysis and follow-through on the job to see that the trainee converts knowledge into skill.

Just as important, you can reinforce the lessons that the trainee can learn elsewhere. Don't act as if company training seminars are time-wasters; instead say, "If only I'd had all these resources when I was starting out in the business. John, I want you to make notes of key issues and share them with me when you get back from training. This old dog would like to learn a few new tricks. Oh, and I'd like to see your action plan telling how you'll use the training back on the job."

PRINCIPLE #5: MENTORS BEGET MENTORS

As valuable as seminars and classes can be, they're just the start. Most learning takes place informally; the water cooler can be the trainer's best friend. Even the lunchroom can.

The wife of a friend works for an educational association, and he tells me that the association does not just consider its people's skills in deciding who gets promoted. No, the group also evaluates how well and how often the employees share their skills. And that's how it should be in the corporate world as well. Make it easy for people to teach other. Tell them, "You won't lose out on a promotion because others learn your skills. Quite the contrary! You'll have leveraged them. You'll be more valuable than ever, and I'll remember when it's time to consider raises."

I can't overemphasize the need for mentors to beget mentors. Don't hide the above five principles from your employees—spread the wisdom around. Let your people know the joys of helping others "Aha" their way to higher performance. After Dawn mentors Joe, a little of her lives on in him forever. Who can rightly resist the chance for this to happen? I feel sorry for Shamu. Whales may take great satisfaction in jumping over the bars, but never will they be able to train others to do the same. That's left to us. Mentoring helps us feel, and be, more human.

ॐ

17

RESPONSIBLE PEOPLE

Gerry Faust, Ph.D
619-536-7970
800-835-0533
faustmgmt@aol.com

Gerry Faust has a wealth of experience. He has founded and led several major companies and held professorships at four universities. (Illinois, Texas, Brigham Young and UCLA) and is a world class speaker and consultant. He is known for his tremendous insight and dynamic and entertaining style of presentation. He is a master story teller whose stories are remembered and make a difference. Dr. Faust is President of Faust Management Corporation, an international management consulting firm that helps businesses and their leaders succeed. He is an expert in business strategy and managing change. Recently he was named the business resource of the year by an internal organization of CEOs. This chapter is an excerpt from his recent best-selling book, *Responsible Managers Get Results:*

How the Best Find Solutions, Not Excuses (with Richard Lyles and Will Phillips—Amacom, 1998).

Gerry Faust is an entrepreneur, behavioral scientist, academician and consultant to a broad range of business, professional and government organizations.

What truly determines success? This question has been studied, written and talked about for centuries. For years psychologists and educators have believed that the Intelligence Quotient (I.Q.) is the strongest determinant of success. Smart people are more likely to be successful. Studies have proved this generally to be true, but the exceptions are numerous. In fact, we now know that intelligence only counts for about twenty percent of the variability in success.

The public speaking circuit has been filled for years with people who have a different answer. "It's attitude that counts," they say. "Think and act like a winner and you will be one" has been their mantra. Recent research has proved they are not far off. But the real answer lies in understanding the specific attitudes, skills and behaviors that determine success.

The recent work on emotional intelligence appears to hold the promise of producing better predictions of success than does I.Q. John Mower, the Yale psychologist who coined the term "emotional intelligence" and Daniel Goleman, who popularized it, describe a variety of qualities they believe are key predictors of success.

Goleman states, "When it comes to predicting people's success braininess as measured by I.Q., standardized achievement tests may actually matter less than the qualities of mind, once thought of as character, before that word began to sound quaint. "

Key factors in emotional intelligence include self-awareness, emotional control, persistence, and the ability to motivate oneself. The research on emotional intelligence has taught us that winners are people who:

1. are aware of their actions and emotions; they know what they are feeling and doing.
2. are able to put off immediate gratification to hold out for more important long-range outcomes.
3. persist in the pursuit of their goals over time and despite adversity.
4. are self-motivating.

But there are other sources of insight on this topic of success. Martin Seligman, a University of Pennsylvania psychologist, has found that optimism, as measured by an instrument he devised, is a fairly accurate predictor of how well a person will succeed in school, sports and many kinds of work.

He has done very well in predicting the success of sales people with his tests. The difference between optimists and pessimists is intriguing. Seligman found that when optimists fail, they most often attribute the failure to something they can control. *Pessimists attribute failure to an innate weakness they are unable to control. Much of the optimists' power comes from their sense of power over their environment.* They believe they make a difference. When optimists succeed, they explain it in terms of permanent causes: traits, abilities or personalities. Pessimists explain success based on chance or temporary conditions, feelings, moods or efforts.

Optimists believe good things are likely to happen again. This confidence is self-reinforcing since it keeps them trying and thinking and problem-solving longer than their pessimistic colleagues. By the way, a lack of confidence is also self-reinforcing. The sales person who believes his calls won't produce results makes fewer calls and produces poorer results.

At Metropolitan Life, Seligman identified optimists who failed on Met Life's standard sales tests and pessimists who performed well on them. Comparing these two groups on the job he found the optimists outsold the pessimists by twenty-one percent the first year and by fifty-seven percent the second. From Seligman we learn that winners:

1. are optimistic.
2. believe they make a difference.
3. believe good things will happen to them.

We might call these winners optimists or people with high E.Q. But if we put it all together we can create an even more powerful conclusion. *Winners are responsible. They believe they make a difference. They are aware of their own feelings and actions. They even stay at difficult tasks to achieve important results. They don't make excuses.*

Responsibility is a concept that has been around for a long time. Although almost everyone recognizes its importance, few truly understand it, its underpinnings or how to create it. *We believe responsibility is the ultimate advantage in a competitive world. For individuals it is the differentiating trait.* It is the trait that all leaders are looking for in their people. For organizations, it's what you rely on after the reengineering, reorganization and process redesign are over. *Responsible people are not relics from the past; rather they are the wave of the future.*

The search throughout the corporate world is for responsible people because they are the ones who produce consistent, high quality results. They are the ultimate competitive weapon for successful businesses in today's fast-changing, results-oriented world.

RESPONSIBILITY DEFINED

There are three important things to remember about responsibility:

1. It is a choice.
2. It means no excuses.
3. It means taking responsibility for producing results.

Responsibility is a personal phenomenon. People can choose to be responsible or not. In fact responsibility is rooted in the fact that no matter what happens to us we are still free to choose what we will think, say and do in a particular situation. We are always able to play the hand no matter what cards we are dealt. This is a very empowering idea—so powerful that it has made survivors and winners out of potential victims for centuries.

The power of this idea is no more graphically demonstrated than by Victor Frankl, who was a Jewish psychiatrist. While imprisoned in Auschwitz, the Nazi death camp, Frankl came to two startling insights that gave him the power to survive and, in fact, to triumph over his captors. He realized that no matter how they treated him, no matter how bad the conditions, the threats, the torture, he still was able to decide what he would say or do. He still had "...the last great human freedom—the freedom to choose." He also found that he could derive the power to succeed from his own dreams, his own vision of his future. The goals he had not yet achieved, the things he desperately wanted to do when the war was over, gave meaning to his life and helped him make daily choices that enabled him to survive. In fact, he found that those who retreated to the past or who wallowed in self-pity did not survive the horrors of Auschwitz, while the people with strong goals and dreams did. He wrote, "Life ultimately means taking the responsibility to find the right answer to its problems and to fulfill the tasks it constantly sets for each individual." Frankl is telling us, in effect, "There is no free lunch" on the great table of life.

Responsible people recognize they have a choice in everything they do. They make the most of the hand they are dealt. Frankl's two great insights can add meaning and power to anyone's life. They are key ingredients in success. They are the stuff that winners are made of. His first insight could be stated:

> It is our goals and dreams for our own future that drive us forward and help us survive and succeed. The power of goals and their relation to success are reflected in the phrase, "When you want what you want more than you don't want to do what it takes to get it, then you will be successful."
>
> More people fail because of the little things they don't want to do than anything else. Some don't want to stay in school. Some don't want to make a tough sales call. Some don't want to confront an unproductive colleague or the facts reflected in their company's financial reports. We all have things we don't want to do. But their "don't wants" fade into nothingness when they stand in the way of clear powerful goals.

Each year I personally go on a vision quest. It happens in the fall in the mountains of southern Utah. Usually it's on a Tuesday. I leave camp with a pack on my back before sunrise and hike for hours. I go to the top of a mountain, to a beautiful spot where you can see for what seems to be hundreds of miles. I catch my breath (a task that takes longer than it did on my first trip eighteen years ago), and there, looking out over the beauty of the mountains, I visit my future.

I close my eyes and mentally go to Faust Management Corporation five years into the future. I talk to the people, attend a management meeting, look at the financials, review the products and plans. I even visit a few customers. I create a clear picture of the future that I want. After my mental visit to the future I write up some notes about what I "saw." These notes are preparation for my personal and company strategic planning, which starts the following month. That vision fills me with hope, conviction, energy and, yes, with some dissatisfaction in the way things are. That vision motivates me to want more and to want "better." It helps me overcome the little things that are getting in the way of greater success.

Make your own vision quest. Power up your life with its energy. Then translate that vision into goals and plans, and you are on your way. You are taking the first steps toward responsibly managing your own success.

Frankl's second great insight can be summed up as:

Life is all about making the most of what you have. No matter what happens, you never lose the ability to decide what to do with the situations you face. You may be experiencing hard times, have little education, have just lost a job or have some physical challenge, but, you never lose your ability to decide what to do next. Winners make those decisions. They choose to do something positive and productive even in the most difficult situations.

Responsibility also means no excuses. Excuses are the opiate of the unsuccessful. There appears to be a worldwide search for excuses today. People blame who they have become on childhood experiences, bad teachers, genetics or lack of education. The problem with excuses is they can become a habit. Once you have the habit, it is easier to find an excuse than to work hard to find a solution. Excuses make people victims, rob them of power, ensure that they lose. Excuses, pessimism and helplessness go hand in hand.

Recently we asked a company CEO why he thought his organization was doing so poorly. He came up with a list of reasons. They included poor location and inadequate marketing, staffing, training and promotion.

We suggested these were problems just waiting to be solved. She agreed and we went to work on them. *The reasons behind one's personal or business problems are best seen as problems to be solved.* Calling them "reasons" can give them the effective power of excuses. *Responsible people create an excuse-free environment. They work hard to lead an excuse-free life.*

RESPONSIBILITY FOR RESULTS

Responsibility can actually be measured on two dimensions represented by two small words: "To" and "For." We start with responsibility to ourselves as infants. The rule is, "Cry if you're unhappy." We soon learn this gets action. When we cry, others come running to take care of what's usually an input or an output problem.

By age two, we hit a crisis when others have had enough of our self-centeredness. At this point responsibility to others begins in earnest. We take on more and more "constituencies" for our responsibility from this time on.

Many believe that as we mature we take on responsibility to others when, actually, it's the other way around: As we take on responsibility to others, we mature.

As we add to our list of those we are responsible to, we add complications to our life. We have to make decisions regarding these responsibilities and often these decisions are difficult and lead to some disappointment. We trade responsibility to the job for responsibility to the family, and the boss is disappointed. Make the trade the other way around and someone else is disappointed. But these are the decisions of life and we must regularly make them.

The "For" dimension of responsibility offers a key insight. There are differing levels of responsibility for each of those we choose to be responsible to. People may be more or less responsible to themselves, their family, their job, their customers, their community.

Most people think of themselves as responsible, but people who are generally judged by others to be more responsible than others take responsibility for results. Those judged less responsible take responsibility for activities. The following example may help to explain this.

On a recent speaking trip to Toronto, I landed in Chicago and raced to the phone. As I called the office I had a vivid *deja vu* experience. Eight years before I had made this same call. When on my way to Toronto to speak at the same conference, I was probably calling from the same terminal and maybe even from the same phone. Eight years ago the phone call had not gone well. At that time I had asked, "Are my materials there yet?" and had been told they had been sent six days earlier. "No" I said, "have they actually arrived?" "Don't worry" was the reply. "I sent them Federal Express." Notice that I was talking results and my colleague was talking activities. This is a critical distinction.

Unnerved by the memory of that call eight years before, I called the office. This time I got a different answer. Amy, my assistant, said, "Don't worry, Alicia got your materials four days ago." They're in good shape. In fact, when I called, she informed me there were 400 extra people coming and when I probed a little further, I found out there could be even more. So I sent 600 extra copies and she received them yesterday."

Now which of these two people would you like to have working for you? I'll take Amy. She knows what results my customers and I want and she makes sure those results happen. She doesn't take the easy way out, she follows through on tasks until she gets results. In a business, successful people are responsible *to* the customers and the organization, and they take responsibility *for* producing the results both customers and the organization want.

If you want to be successful in your job or in your business, focus on developing an understanding of the results wanted by customers and the organization. Then take on and get others to take on responsibility for those results.

Inevitably, most job descriptions don't focus on results. They focus on activities and therefore do not help in creating their desired focus. All too often managers' comments to employees, and their criticism and feedback focus on activities rather than results.

RESPONSIBLE MANAGERS RELY ON RESPONSIBLE PEOPLE

They provide goals and objectives and teach them the difference between great results and average performance. They help their colleagues develop the skills needed to produce the desired results and then they get out of the way to let them succeed.

Workers want this kind of leadership because above all else, they are motivated by meaningful work. That is, they are motivated by work in which the desired goals are defined, the boundaries of performance (including core values and key policies) are understood, and where they must use their talent, skills, judgment and problem-solving abilities to produce the desired results. The joy in work comes in accomplishing important, yet difficult things and in which your efforts made a difference.

Responsible people are results-oriented, problem-solvers. They solve problems for themselves, their organization and the customer. They work in an uncertain world, as we all do, but they get joy from accomplishing difficult things, where others might choose to use an excuse. Responsible people are winners. They are the most "in demand" commodity in today's complex and fast-moving world.

Responsible people don't just take responsibility for doing things, they understand the goals (desired results) and they choose to take responsibility for producing those results.

Responsible people are problem-solvers. They have to be because things go wrong. When that happens responsible people don't make excuses—they start problem solving.

৪০

18

COACHES, ROLLER COASTERS & OPPORTUNITY

Jim Clack
800-633-7762
910-282-6303
SALES@Brooksgroup.com

Jim Clack is a thirteen-year veteran NFL lineman, an All-Pro, and a recipient of two Super Bowl Rings. He was a star performer for the Super Bowl Champion Pittsburgh Steelers for nine years and subsequently Captain of the New York Giants for four years. Jim is President of The Brooks Group, a full-service speaking, training and consulting firm located in Greensboro, NC. Jim Clack's story has touched thousands of people and encouraged them to achieve and continue to strive in spite of their own personal obstacles.

There is a direct parallel between life and a roller coaster. They both have tremendous highs and heart-stopping lows. In both cases, it feels like you'll never reach the top, while the inevitable trip to the bottom can be fast, furious, unpredictable and chaotic. The difference is that roller coasters are supposed to be fun. The roller coaster of life can often be less than fun-filled.

One of the characteristics that often separates high achievers from everyone else is the drive and willingness to begin the long, circuitous climb back up—time after time. Being on top is a long-term goal. The challenge is how you weather the route to the next pinnacle and maneuver the pitfalls that crop up against your staying there.

Those people who are most successful are the ones who overcome burdensome setbacks and obstacles. They are also the ones who are able to maintain clear direction (focus), know they cannot succeed alone (teamwork) and are totally driven to achieve personal goals (commitment). Even with an understanding of these three elements of success, far too many people still place a self-generated governor on the belief that they can achieve their full potential.

If a person does maintain the strict inner belief that he or she can succeed, there is a mysterious, almost magnetic power that somehow draws significant others into their lives to assist them in their journey.

Opportunities to fight back to the top always seem to surface through circumstances, relationships and alliances with others who somehow come into your life.

My first setback occurred in 1963. My father, Linwood Clack, passed away unexpectedly at the young age of 47. This was particularly shocking for a high school sophomore who had grown to love, admire and respect his balanced combination of harsh discipline and fair judgment. My father's expectations were high and his support unparalleled. His belief in his son was unmatched.

The week before his untimely death, my father was able to see me score the winning basket in the final game of the North Carolina State Basketball Championships. He made the 260-mile round-trip in one day despite a severe, rapidly onsetting illness.

Upon my return from the game, I spotted my dad on our front porch proudly cutting up fifty copies of our local paper with the bold headline, "Jim Clack Wins State Championship" and sending all fifty to friends and relatives. Unfortunately, he passed away fewer than five days later. To this very day, thirty-five years later, I still picture him surrounded with those articles that he so lovingly and pridefully clipped and sent.

Needless to say, in the span of several short weeks I went from the pinnacle of success to the depths of despair. During that short but traumatic period of time, I just about gave up hope for any meaningful future. I knew that, financially, college was out of the question. It was no secret that my future was quickly slipping away from me.

That was until Henry Trevathen, my football and track coach, took me under his wing and, in essence, became my second father. He was also my guiding light, advisor, mentor, confidante and teacher. Following his advice and counsel I was able to obtain athletic and academic rewards that exceeded even my wildest dreams.

Scores of athletic scholarships came my way. I found myself in the enviable position of being able to pick and choose from hundreds of college opportunities from coast-to-coast. I know my father was looking down at me and Coach Trevathen was looking right at me, both urging me to make the right decision.

After a successful college career at Wake Forest, my second great opportunity came along. Along with that opportunity came the next two people to impact my life. They were Art Rooney, Sr. (owner of the Steelers) and Chuck Noll (newly named coach of the Steelers). I was a 214-pound free-agent lineman with a gigantic $500 signing bonus in 1969, when the Steelers were at the lowest ebb in the history of franchises. Comparing that $500 to today's salaries is like comparing the corner store to Wal-Mart!

Even at that low point for the Steelers, I was not able to make the team in 1969. Nor in 1970. Not even in 1971! But I did eventually make the squad, thanks in no small measure to Mr. Rooney's belief in me and Coach Noll's patience and willingness to work tirelessly with me.

Thirteen years later I had played nine years at center and guard for the Steelers. I had started in two Super Bowls and was the proud owner of two Super Bowl rings. I also played four years with the New York Giants where I was team captain and made the All-Pro Team at center for three years.

The truth is that professional football can, unfortunately, be a fantasy world. My first awakening to the real world began on the evening of July 17, 1985 when my wife and I were involved in a horrendous automobile accident. Fortunately, she sustained injuries that were treatable and she was released several days later.

I wasn't nearly as lucky. I was pinned in the car for two hours. The intensive care unit was my home for two weeks. I spent another month in the hospital. Several more months were spent in rehabilitation with specialists who taught me how to walk, speak, eat and return to relative normality. Yet, even today I still suffer pain and discomfort from that accident.

The enormous amount of time and focused attention that I had to place on my physical recovery diverted my attention from my previously flourishing restaurants. Without my day-to-day involvement, these, too, took a dramatic slide and it wasn't long until my financial situation got as dismal as my health had been.

As the old saying goes, "I got so poor I couldn't pay attention!" Then, in 1988, I found myself seated among a group of retired NFL players at a Florida resort hotel uncertain of what to do next with my life. Something unique happened to me that day as I found myself riveted by a speaker who was telling us how we, as former players, could bring a tremendous amount of positive influence to others through corporate speaking, training and consulting. We could help thousands of people by relating our own stories in conjunction with meaningful, powerful ideas.

The speaker that day, Bill Brooks, would become my fifth coach—the fifth person who helped me find a route out of despair and impending failure. I made up my mind that the speaking, training and consulting profession was where my future would be. It would be the avenue for me to make my way back to the pinnacle.

The problem? Bill had no need for additional staff. But I had already learned the hard lesson of how to ask, to be patient and to ask again. The worst that could happen would be a series of "No's"! I was dogged, determined and deliberate in my attempt to enter this exciting field.

Two months later Bill asked if I'd be interested in being part of a video program he was developing for one of his highly visible, important clients. He was willing to take a chance on me and I was willing to take a chance on my ability to deliver.

I can still vividly recall what happened after that grueling, two-day video shoot. Bill came into the studio and said, "Jim, you have a lot of work to do, but I can see you're both determined and coachable. That's a rare combination. How about coming to work at our firm?"

Ten years later, I became president of Bill's organization. But that was really the result of five hard-driving, demanding and perfectionistic coaches: Linwood Clack, Chuck Noll, Art Rooney, Henry Trevathen and Bill Brooks.

Over the past three years I have delivered more than 400 programs. I have been able to touch thousands of people. I'm not back on top yet, but my work has instilled in me a belief that I will be. It's just a matter of time. My personal, financial, spiritual and professional growth are back on track.

My total belief in the power of Focus, Teamwork and Commitment has provided the opportunity. But other people and their belief in me have really been the fuel that has made all of it possible.

It is your challenge to provide the spark that will get the attention of your coaches. They will then coach you to greatness. But always remember that in order for this to be possible you must be "coachable." You see, life is a two-way street in which success and failure can go in either direction.

Even the greatest coaches cannot make an unwilling player successful. It's up to you to attract your coach, be willing to work hard and then fulfill your potential. In order to do this, there are three guiding principles worth following. And worth following to the letter:

- Set exciting goals.
- Become committed to your beliefs.
- Exhibit to others that you are willing to stay committed, be coachable and reciprocate with time, effort and energy.

Stay focused on these principles and the right people will come into your life, too. Call them coaches, mentors, leaders, teachers or role models. Regardless of their titles, they will help you achieve more than you ever could on your own.

℘

19

A LIFE MORE DECATHLON THAN MARATHON

Don Hutson,
CSP, CPAE
800-647-9166
901-767-0000
DLHutson@aol.com

George H. Lucas,
Ph.D.
800-647-9166
901-767-0000
DLHutson@aol.com

Don Hutson has been featured in more than eighty training films for American industry, he has appeared before more than two-thirds of the Fortune 500 Companies. He is regularly featured on both the Public Broadcasting Station and the TPN

Satellite Network. Don is a past president of the National Speakers Association and a recipient of the prestigious "Cavett Award."

George Lucas is the author of several leading business books, including *Retailing, Marketing Strategy and Plans, Marketing Strategy Text and Cases, Strategic Marketing Management* and *The Alliance Initiative* co-authored with Don Hutson. George is President of U. S. Learning and is based in Memphis, TN.

The Olympic Decathlon is truly an extraordinary event. It encompasses ten events from both track and field. Winners must be strong and skilled, and run with both speed and endurance. While we both marvel at anyone who can run more than twenty-six miles to complete a marathon, it is largely a singular task to be a marathoner rather than a decathlete and, for this reason, the gold medalist in the decathlon is widely regarded as the world's greatest athlete.

It is not our purpose here to debate the challenge presented by various sporting events but, rather, to draw a clear parallel between the multitude of diverse events facing an Olympic decathlete and the day-to-day challenges people face in their increasingly complex lives. While the decathlete competes in ten events, each of us must fill a comparable number of roles in our lives. We have found that comparing these roles to "wearing hats" adds clarity to the process of understanding the complex and often conflicting paths each of us must follow on a daily or weekly basis. Father/mother, husband/wife, son/daughter, neighbor, youth sports coach, church committee member, volunteer for the United Way or Scout leader, and last, but not anything close to least, employee (boss/colleague/subordinate).

Yet, while the decathlete has a training regimen and a schedule of events over the two days of competition, most of us go through life without any real plan and often resemble a ceiling fan's blades as we change "hats" from moment to moment without any advance warning.

Today's truly great leaders understand that you don't just lead employees, you lead people, and people have many components to their lives, one of the most important of which is family.

One of the most important ways leaders can inspire others to win is to help them bring balance and coordination to their many life roles. This does not happen naturally or easily. Were that the case the divorce rate would not be fifty percent, the number of family counselors would not be growing exponentially and employee burn-out would not be at an all time high.

Most successful organizations today have well-developed and documented strategic plans that assess and drive the direction of various strategic business units (SBUs).

With the increasing complexity of life today, having more roles with more resource demands on an often stagnant or shrinking resource base, successful competitors in the events of life must have a comprehensive strategic plan as well. This plan must address all their key roles, or what we call SLUs (strategic life units). The days when leaders could simply take the stance that, "What you do on your own time is your business," went by the wayside as drug and alcohol testing became commonplace. What employees and colleagues do in their nonwork SLUs often *does* significantly reduce their ability to win the gold. Just as there is an interdependence among SBUs in a firm, the SLUs of an individual also are highly dependent on one another.

In the phases that follow, we will lay out a structure for personal strategic planning that you and your associates can utilize. It is similar to the model for corporate strategic planning taught in most business schools, and practiced by managers in the Fortune 1000 companies as well as in successful smaller organizations.

The process that you will be exposed to is one we have repeatedly tested, refined and proven with participants ranging from high school students to board chairmen.

THE PERSONAL STRATEGIC PLANNING MODEL

Just as preparation for an Olympic decathlon should be structured and coordinated, to get the most from the time and effort we put into personal strategic planning, it should also follow a logically sequenced set of steps or phases. Each phase should be simple enough that we don't end up just planning instead of living our life. The quality of each phase is heavily dependent on the successful completion of the preceding phase(s). These phases are:

1. The personal SWOT (strengths, weaknesses, opportunities and threats) Analysis that considers both you and your environment;
2. Personal Mission Statement development and refinement (this step should be means-focused, not ends-focused);

3. Developing Personal Goals and Objectives as outcome targets for all SLUs;
4. Strategy Identification for goal and objective achievement;
5. Budgeting Time and other Resources for selected personal strategies; and
6. Personal strategic plan Implementation and Evaluation and Control

PHASE 1: YOUR PERSONAL *SWOT* ANALYSIS

The personal strategic planning process must begin with a comprehensive reflection on one's internal and external environments. The strengths and weaknesses internal component of SWOT deals with factors that are largely within our control. They are traits and characteristics that describe and define us. We are convinced that the most successful people in life tend to be those who identify their strengths and build on them as their foundation for success. They also do something else that is not nearly as enjoyable. They identify their weaknesses and then do all they can to eliminate the ones they can and, at least, competently manage those that they cannot totally eliminate.

It is not uncommon now for people to downplay the importance of their own traits in determining their successes. These life participants have a high degree of a factor know as external locus, or source of control. Life medalists generally have a high *internal* locus of control, as they see their level of success being largely determined by their own strengths and weaknesses.

Internal locus of control is apparant in a quote from one of the United States' most famous Olympic decathlon champions, Bruce Jenner in Charlie Jones' book, *What Makes Winners Win*. Here he states:

"I determine my future. I don't let anything on the outside of me determine my future. I'm in control. The crowd doesn't have anything to do with it, other competitors don't have anything to do with it, the jet flying overhead doesn't have anything to do with it. If I'm going to do well, it's going to come from inside me."

As you complete the internal portion of your SWOT, recognize that it is not uncommon for an aspect that is a strength in one part of our lives to also be a weakness in another SLU. Being a "workaholic" may produce positive short-term results in the job SLU, but can be a significant detriment to several other roles. You should also be careful to note where you stand at the present time on each factor, not where you hope to be at some later point.

A partial list of the factors that you may want to address for your different life roles would include:

- self-confidence
- reading participation and comprehension
- honesty/ethics
- teamwork
- leadership skills
- family support
- listening skills
- written communication skills
- verbal communication skills
- foreign language fluency
- sense of humor
- faith
- travel/life experience
- financial resources/stability, health/energy/exercise
- follow-up/follow-through tendencies

Even with our total endorsement of having and coaching an internal locus of control mindset, there are external factors that must be monitored and addressed for each SLU. These factors comprise the opportunities and threats portion of the SWOT. Such factors are largely outside our control, but they nonetheless impact our daily lives. These factors combine to create an external environment that can help or hinder our efforts to be successful in all SLUs.

You can be proactive, reactive, or inactive regarding your external environment—and the failure to anticipate or recognize an external environment issue effectively rules out the most preferred proactive option. Many individuals have become stressed-out in their attempt to control these uncontrollables. Let's not try to achieve the impossible, but simply benefit from a clear awareness of these factors so we might develop a more viable strategic plan. Successful decathletes would not let the weather determine if they won or lost a competition, but they would most certainly monitor the forecast and plan their pace and equipment accordingly.

A sample list of external factors that you may want to address in your SWOT include, but are not limited to:

- current attitudes and behaviors of others
- the local, regional, and national economy
- technological innovations
- the legal environment
- social issues/values
- local and global competition
- your company's training and support programs

PHASE 2: DEVELOPING YOUR PERSONAL MISSION STATEMENT

With the completion of your SWOT, you are now ready to develop the most important component of your personal strategic plan—your mission statement. This piece of anyone's plan should tell everyone who reads it:

- Who you are
- What is important to you
- What you stand for
- What your values are
- How you "operate" as a person

It must address all SLUs in your life: Family, career, social, spiritual, etc., and it should be the most permanent part of your personal strategic plan.

The construction of a personal mission statement is not an easy task. Your first draft should take at least twenty minutes to complete, and in all likelihood, several editions of your mission statement will be required to get to the point where you feel comfortable enough about a draft to share it with other people who are important in your life. This should be the first thing you ask someone you are directing to develop a plan to share with you.

In assessing the appropriateness of your mission statement, only you can determine the content issues, but the following criteria should help you in developing one that is of maximum value. Your mission statement should be:

1. Means-focused as opposed to ends-focused
2. Comprehensive in that it addresses all critical aspects of your life
3. In line with your present (or anticipated) strengths and weaknesses
4. Consistent with how you think key others view you in your SLUs

5. A statement you take pride in and feel comfortable using as your plan's cornerstone

The purpose of your mission statement is to fortify you in times of crisis, center you in times of success and direct you when you face critical decisions.

We said earlier that before you can teach, you first must learn. To show you that we heed our own doctrine, and to give you a little more direction in the development of your own mission statement, our own present mission statements follow.

> To put forth creative energy to enhance the quality of life for myself, family members, associates, and clients in any way possible. I will strive to learn, to grow, to progress, and to excel in my chosen endeavors. I will remain committed to God and my religious beliefs and keep them sacred. I will maintain a win-win spirit in every relationship I choose to be a part of. I will always make it a priority to be a positive and energizing influence not only on other people, but in my community.
>
> —Don Hutson

> In my family and personal roles as husband, father, son, brother (in-law), uncle, and friend it is crucial that I be as loving, supportive, caring, and nurturing as possible. I believe that life itself is exceedingly valuable, and thus each day should be seen as a blessing from God of which I should make the most. In working with clients and colleagues, and in the community, I strive to be a true educator, not just a speaker or trainer, and to be positive, professional, ethical, enlightening, and a productive team player in doing all that I do in the highest quality fashion. In that opportunity costs are always the highest costs, I strive to chose and follow my paths wisely.
>
> —George Lucas

PHASE 3: DEVELOPING GOALS AND OBJECTIVES

Now that you have at least a draft of your mission statement, you are in solid position to begin identifying what ends you hope to accomplish for each of your SLUs. The achievement of such goals and objectives is only possible through successfully "living" our mission statement. Our experiences have shown that even though most people recognize that writing down a goal or an objective dramatically increases the probability that it will be realized, people are reluctant to take this step. A variety of reasons are given, but time is the most frequently heard excuse. We question whether this is the true reason for the inactivity. More likely causes of failure to take this simple step are the fear of failure, questioning whether one deserves the outcome, and not adequately assessing the pros and cons associated with each objective. The truth is that getting our goals and objectives in writing enhances not only our commitment to them, but triples the probability of achieving these outcomes.

Experience has shown that people tend to live up to the expectations of their leaders, managers, or mentors. Expect little in the way of outcomes, and that is what will be obtained. We strongly endorse our friend and author Jerry Bresser's more productive approach, which is that there are no unrealistic goals, only unrealistic *time frames*.

For best results, we see Phase Three as a two-step process, with goal-setting coming before objective setting. Step one should involve the establishment of at least one general target or goal for each of your critical life roles. Goals tend to be more general and have a longer time frame associated with them.

Goals should be:

1. consistent with the other goals in your set (earning a graduate degree or starting a new business and spending more time with one's family are not consistent if set for a simultaneous time frame)
2. realistic given your present SWOT (foreign language proficiency would be a plus for a colleague seeking an international assignment, for example)
3. rigorous enough to drive an increase in your SLU performance (serving on or chairing a fund-raising drive for a children's hospital is preferable to just joining the organization that is conducting the drive)
4. driven by your personal mission statement (the process of developing your personal mission statement should bring several areas where performance should be enhanced to light)

Once your goal set has been developed, you now must get specific in terms of how you will chart progress toward the accomplishment of these goals. This is why we like separating phase three into two steps. Those people who do put targets to writing tend to do so in very general terms that don't force them to hold their feet to the fire (e.g., "Do a better job with my kids"). We call these more specific progress checkpoints "objectives." As with goals, well-constructed objectives meet a set of standards. They are:

1.   stated in definite and quantitative terms (e.g., Save $400 a month in a college account for my child's education.)

2.   tied to a starting and ending date (e.g., Starting next month and continuing for three months, I will read to my child for thirty minutes each night.)

3.   assigned a clear priority (e.g., My No. 1 objective for the month is to get commitments from three new customers.)

4.   assigned a system for regular progress review (e.g., daily, weekly or monthly, appropriate with the length of time for the objective; that is, daily for a weekly objective)

PHASE 4: STRATEGY IDENTIFICATION

While your goals and objectives may look good to you on paper, will you really make them happen? Without a clear direction for goal and objective accomplishment, most people will fail to meet their targets, and then quickly decide that goal and objective setting is just "a waste of time."

As you review your targeted outcomes, or those of another, one fundamental question must be asked, "Will the status quo get you there?" The answer to this question will direct you to the development of one of two strategy types; (1) continuance strategies or (2) change strategies.

Continuance strategies are put in place to direct you in continuing to build on the strengths identified in your SWOT to take fullest advantage of your environment. You should note that a continuance strategy is not the failure to develop a strategy. It is focused and deliberate. Without such strategies your strengths may start to become neglected, and even turn into weaknesses. Continuance strategies are appropriate when continuing on the same level of improvement. Your trend line will deliver on the goals and objectives you developed.

For example, if you are saving $400 a month for your child's education, with the objective of reaching a carefully calculated amount by the time your eight-year-old reaches college age (and you don't plan on having more children), the strategy would be this:

Continue your present savings rate in this goal area of providing for a college education through the objective of saving $400 a month to a designated account.

A key point to keep in mind is that with continuance strategies, only the strategy remains the same, not the outcome. You remain on the trend line as that college account continues to grow each and every month from the deposit, plus accrued interest.

Conversely, change strategies identify the weaknesses that must be avoided, managed or, preferably, converted into strengths for positive results. Simply put, a continuation of what you are presently doing just won't get you there. For example, you have a goal of moving into a management position within your company and you recognize one of your weaknesses is the lack of a graduate degree, which is a requirement for advancement in your company.

In this situation, you have three strategic options. You can continue to blame the "system" for continually overlooking your superior abilities at promotion time; you can drop your goal of advancement into management and live happily at your present level, (perhaps telling yourself, "Managers have to deal with too many hassles anyway, why do I need that?") or you can accept a strategy of returning to night classes to earn an MBA. This goal and strategy would be combined with an objective of completing the admissions test with a satisfactory score within six months from today.

A third option besides avoidance or conversion that is increasingly being utilized today to overcome weaknesses is to bring in an alliance partner who has a compensating strength. Neither of us is particularly skilled in managing computer systems. We utilize an individual who understands our needs and configures our systems to keep us productive.

PHASE 5: BUDGETING TIME AND OTHER RESOURCES

In undertaking the strategies outlined in Phase Four, a major challenge we all face is insufficient resources. The failure to identify and manage the consumption of key resources is a major reason people fail to experience victory in life.

There are at least four key resource pools that must be managed and allocated in keeping with your strategies:

1. Your *time*
2. Your *money and financial resources*

3. Your *tools* (e.g., equipment, computers and other support materials)
4. Your personal *network*

All four resource pools have the ability to drive or restrict our performance or that of a colleague or friend we are directing.

As we work with salespeople in training programs, we are constantly amazed at how many of them lack the proper tools to achieve their sales objectives concerning promotion, recognition or compensation. They often lack computers, pagers, cellular phones or some other tool to create more substantial customer relationships. When questioned about this resource gap, they usually go external in their locus of control and blame their organization for failing to provide the item. Yet they usually are aware that they can easily cover the cost of a cell phone multiple times with the additional commissions they would generate.

One way we have found to overcome this personal resource limitation is to create a *personal development budget*. This budget should embody all the financial expenditures necessary to implement our identified strategies. It can include funds for computers, compensation for alliance partners (including gifts and dinners for friends who help you out), education, books, magazine subscriptions and even our vacations.

This budget does two things for our personal strategic planning. First, it increases the probability that when funds are needed they will be available. Second, it reduces the guilt or concern that is so frequently experienced when the money is expended. Encourage the people you work with to start such an account, after you have done so yourself. Start small (e.g., $50 a month) and build over time as you see the return on the resources invested. This evokes the old adage, "It takes money to make money."

As we stated at the beginning of this phase, it is not just our money that must be budgeted, but other resources must be carefully allocated, too. When any change strategy is set there will be a significant impact on other areas. Frequently, something must be given up entirely or its priority status reduced. Going back to school to get an MBA has a significant two- to four-year impact on one's career and family time. This should not be minimized, and must be viewed as an investment with returns for the other SLUs. Keep in mind that the failure to do budget or allocate resources can have significant consequences for this strategy and our other strategies as well.

PHASE 6: IMPLEMENTATION, EVALUATION AND CONTROL

In this phase of our plan, you work out the details, start carrying out strategies and monitor your progress in investing your resources and achieving your objectives as you live your mission statement. Several concerns must be addressed at this point to get the maximum benefit from your strategic plan. First, you must keep your plan alive and active. Quick daily and weekly reviews of your objectives and resource allocations should take place. On a monthly basis more formal objective evaluations should occur. If the objective is not reached, was it realistic in light of the resources we could mobilize, and/or the environment that unfolded? Perhaps the level was set too high. Reading to your child five nights a week when you are frequently gone on business three or four nights each week is not a flaw in personal strategic planning or the objective category, but in the level that was established. Perhaps additional unanticipated job responsibilities came along. This change requires us to revisit all of our objectives, as well as our resource budget allocation decisions.

Just as important is what we do when an objective is achieved. *Successful people find ways to reward themselves for objective accomplishment.* If you are looking for someone else to reward you, prepare for regular disappointment. In *The Olympians Guide to Winning the Game of Life* cited earlier, Daley Thompson of Great Britain, who won the gold in the decathlon in both 1980 and 1984, states, "My enjoyment obviously comes from winning, but more than anything else it comes from performing well. I think that, having performed well, I wouldn't mind coming in second or third. Because at the end of the day, I'm the only one I really have to please."

When you please yourself with objective achievement, reward yourself. It may be just a pat on the back, a more tangible reward such as a nicer tie or scarf than you would normally buy, or a fine piece of art work you have had your eye on. *The nature of the reward is less important than the event.* It should just be something you value. Every time you think of it or look at it you will know that you achieved something meaningful.

At this point, so many people lose their commitment to personal planning and to their personal plan. Don't let it become like those hollow New Year's resolutions that so frequently are broken before the Super Bowl or even the Orange Bowl is over. Stick with what is working. Take corrective steps regarding those things that are not working. Regularly tweak and fine-tune your game plan. Keep your planning simple and fun so you look forward to the one minute at the end of the day, five minutes at the end of the week and the ten minutes at the end of the month when you review and refine your plan. In keeping with the theme of this book, share your plan with others and invite them to do likewise with you. Our best mentors are those who know and remind us of our objectives and share with us in their accomplishment.

CONCLUDING THOUGHTS

It has been said that most people can be categorized as either winners or whiners. While this sounds simplistic, we are convinced that which of the two categories that people fall into is the result of a set of decisions and not a random occurrence. We must control our behavior, our attitude and our success plan. Winners take charge! Your internalized motivation and resulting proactive behavior will result in you getting a bigger bite out of life. On at least an annual basis, you should set aside time to revise Phase One, the personal SWOT, and carefully evaluate all phases for any changes that may be necessary. As you consider whether you should begin a personal strategic plan for yourself, the words of an old mentor come to mind, "Do you have a plan, or are you just part of someone else's plan." People who lack such direction are likely to become an unwitting part of the resource budget of those who have a clear plan for their lives. As you begin this process, naturally questioning whether it will deliver the value we have promised, keep one last adage in mind:

Those people who believe they can and
Those people who believe they can't both are probably right!

∞

20

THE ROLE OF ROLE MODELS

Bill Brooks,
CSP, CPAE
800-633-7762
910-282-6303
SALES@Brooksgroup.com

Bill Brooks is a former college football coach and president of a national $300 million sales organization. He is the author of eight books, and has produced more than 100 video programs and 200 audio programs. Bill has been featured in *USA Today, Selling, Selling Power, The Wall Street Journal* and other trade and professional journals worldwide. He has spoken to more than 1,500 CEOs as well as to the NFL Players Association.

Bill Brooks serves on the Board of Directors for the Psycho-Cybernetics Foundation and is CEO of the Brooks Group, a full-service speaking, training and consulting firm.

Perhaps the very first question that needs to be addressed with reference to Role Models is a two-pronged, but very simple one: Who and where are they?

There is little argument that any individual who models certain behaviors, values, beliefs and actions can impact others who aspire to the same lifestyle.

Our society is filled with people who are labeled as coaches, managers, mentors and leaders. Literature and research are loaded with data and systems for mentoring and managing. The real truth is that simple, straightforward modeling of correct behaviors is at the very core of all of these issues. Unfortunately, role modeling is given far too little attention, if not completely avoided, except in an occasional college sociology text.

There is little doubt that human beings are both psychologically and sociologically influenced. Each of us lives in a world surrounded by other human beings. There is little disagreement about the view that people tend to become very much like those with whom they associate.

In recent memory lots of high profile role models in our society have tended to fall into the arenas of sports, politics, entertainment and the media. The problem? A growing lack of acceptance on the part of many of these people regarding the role that "goes with the territory." Often, there is an outright refusal to exhibit the behavior expected of serious role models. Even worse, it would appear that all too often the personal behavior of these people has nothing to do with their professional roles. Essentially, then, we cheer on the least attractive characteristics. Arguments such as: "The issues are more important than the personalities" are the products of highly paid spin doctors, athletes who are overpaid and under-committed, politicians who blatantly promise all things to all people (and whose private lives rarely match their public personas), and entertainers who flaunt lifestyles that are less-than-admirable. The list goes on with bad example after bad example. Just check your local news any evening. The lead stories speak for themselves.

The good news is that role models still do come from the ranks of everyday people. Unfortunately, through the help of mass media, huge public relations budgets and slick spokespersons, the wrong people are (1) seen as role models, (2) abandon the responsibility that this carries, and (3) are protected when they do it.

Given these realities, let's take a hard look at the functions of a role model. Ideally, such a person would consistently exhibit the characteristics that another may aspire to emulate, assimilate, internalize and eventually adopt.

Traditionally, this person may have been a coach or a teacher—perhaps a parent or a relative. It may have been a colleague or a superior. In each case, however, this person actually was (as opposed to only appearing to be) the type of person you would have wanted to emulate or become—the type of person that you would be proud to be.

The most perplexing component of everyday role models is that the role is often based on a perception that can be eroded all too easily because the "average" role model doesn't have spin doctors, pundits or protectors to defend their actions. Unfortunately, it can take one isolated incident or unguarded moment to eradicate the image others hold of that person. That means that there is no downtime for a role model.

Given the obvious need for role models, the underachieving cast of players who are our contemporary role models, as well as the fragility of the role, let's examine the twelve most essential characteristics of positive, effective role models.

1. They understand that others expect a certain standard of behavior from them based on role, position or circumstance.
    This is taken freely and lived up to daily. Serious role models understand the microscope under which they operate.

2. They are willing to accept the role that has been cast upon them.
    This is done of free-will and total acceptance. A failure to accept the mantle that has been placed on you is pure abdication of the role.

3. They are capable of exhibiting the correct behaviors, attitudes, skills and values that are consistent with the role they have chosen to play.
    This is not an uncomfortable role. In other words, they are able to live their role...walk their talk...with no hesitancy or inconsistency.

4. They understand that being a role model is a full-time, twenty-four-hour-a-day role.

This means no downtime—ever. There is no such thing as letting your guard down. There is no room for a second-best behavior.

5. They realize the long-term value and benefit of role modeling to others.
This is a process that occurs over time rather than as a one-time event. They understand that this is giving to others at its best and that it requires a commitment of time.

6. They work at self-improvement in every facet of their own lives.
This is the process of becoming an ever better role model by continuously improving every facet of life.

7. They monitor the impact that their actions have on others—positive or negative.
There is constant and accurate course correction as needed.

8. They are willing to allow those modeling their behavior to grow and, quite often, surpass the role model.
This goes far beyond personal ego. Rather, it goes to the selflessness of personal sacrifice that says, "Yes, I am willing to let you grow beyond me....no strings attached."

9. They understand that regardless of the situation, consistency is the most essential characteristic of role model behavior.
This is based on a steady and planned process that incorporates every facet of life. It requires careful intention not to give even the impression of any impropriety.

10. They understand that there are three consistent and specific characteristics that translate into any role model situation. These are:

Honesty
Integrity
Commitment

11. They accept that it is impossible to positively impact everyone.
This means that some who emulate the role model will fail. They understand that everyone has the right to fail, however, they believe that to fail to try is simply a lack of sufficient effort.

12. They take their role seriously and consistently ask themselves, "How will this action be perceived by those who see me as a role model?"
This means there is a constant awareness of the role and a consistent effort to fulfill the behaviors expected of that role.

By the same token, those who choose to internalize and emulate role models also have some basic rules by which they need to operate as well. Here they are:

1. You can never be someone else nor should you ever try. You can only be yourself.
2. Accept yourself for what you are—and what you are not.
3. Identify those characteristics you most want to emulate and find someone who not only exhibits those characteristics, but actually lives them to the very core of their being.
4. Accept that the person you have chosen to be your role model is a human being, which means that there will be weaknesses and inadequacies. Don't expect perfection.
5. Let the person know why you chose them to be your role model. Tell them how much you appreciate their efforts and what characteristics they possess that made you choose them.
6. Work to become a role model yourself.

What about the pressure this puts on those who choose to be (or are chosen) role models? Unfortunately, lots of people are selected to be role models, whether they personally choose the role or not. These role models are present in every city, town and rural area in the world. They are men, women and children who are nameless and faceless to much of the world.

Unfortunately, this also means that there are lots of everyday people who are negative role models too. Some examples? Parents whose idea of a relationship embodies domestic strife and conflict, including the father who drifts from job to job and the mother who abandons her children. It includes the sales manager who cheats on expense reports, the employer who mistreats employees, the Little League coach who wants to win at all costs, the older sibling who teaches the younger siblings to drink and use drugs.

Often, there is little pressure exerted on these negative role models. At least not immediately. It does, however, become cumulative over time as the behavior fueled by these negative influences is manifested in later years by those who go on to emulate the very same behavior they have witnessed.

What is the potential result? A generation of liars, cheaters, drug abusers and deadbeats. That is when the pressure really builds—on society, including employers, police departments, school systems, jails and all the rest.

The short-term pressure to perform lies with those who choose to control their behaviors, do what is right, be a person worth emulating and a person willing to put pressure on oneself to be the type of person they would want others to emulate.

The real questions are these: Why should there be role models? Is it really that important? Here are the answers:

1. We have no choice. People are influenced by other people. The more influential that person is, the greater the power.

2. It really is that important. Just as norms, expectations and values are handed down from generation to generation, so are individual ways of behaving, treating others, meeting obligations and all the other behaviors that society exhibits.

The bottom line is simple. It is the responsibility of all people, one person at a time, to take responsibility for their own actions and, subsequently, to be accountable for accepting the fact that they do influence other people. That there are others who are influenced by what sociologists call "significant others." Who are these significant others? Among others, they include:

- Professional peers
- Factory workers
- Professional supervisors
- Steelworkers
- Community leaders
- Salespeople
- Parents
- Teachers

- Coaches
- Pilots
- Doctors
- Clerks
- Lawyers
- Dentists
- Technicians
- You, me...all of us!

And some more:

- Felons
- Dishonest public officials
- Some professional athletes

- Liars
- Some celebrities
- Cheaters

The question is this: Which role models are more positive? By the same token, which ones have the most influence on the most people? Interesting question, isn't it? The answers are even more interesting.